"Most unusual insight[...] *opened my mind and*[...] *come alive. A must read for those who want to be on the cutting edge of vital 21st century issues."*

– GERALD COATES, founder of Pioneer, speaker, author and broadcaster

"A fresh and intriguing approach to the figure of Jesus in the Gospels. It is widely recognized that Jesus scandalized some of his contemporaries, especially the religious elite, but Instone-Brewer takes this idea much further. He draws on his extensive knowledge of rabbinic literature to show us in detail how much of Jesus' behaviour and teaching must have appeared shocking. But Instone-Brewer wears his learning lightly. His lively style and the parallels he draws with our own society will appeal to a wide range of readers.

– PROFESSOR RICHARD BAUCKHAM, FBA, FRSE

"A thought-provoking book packed with background material that is both well-researched and well written. It brings new colours to the Gospels and helps explain the scandalous teaching and behaviour of Jesus. Read it and see why the gospel is called 'good news.'"

– IAN COFFEY, author and teacher

"Applied theology at its best – a scholar painstakingly working to understand the thought-world of the first century New Testament, and a pastor painstakingly applying its message to a whole host of twenty-first century problems. Written in an accessible, engaging and appropriately humorous style... you will be illumined, challenged and immensely helped. Highly recommended!"

– DR STEVE BRADY, Principal, Moorlands College, Christchurch

Revd Dr David Instone-Brewer is a Baptist Minister who was seconded to the academic world by his denomination. He is now the Senior Research Fellow in Rabbinics and the New Testament at Tyndale House in Cambridge. He has written several academic books and articles on early Judaism and the Bible, as well as regular contributions to *Christianity* magazine. Other interests include computer programming and lowbrow movies.

THE JESUS SCANDALS

Why he shocked his contemporaries (and still shocks today)

DAVID INSTONE-BREWER

MONARCH
BOOKS

Oxford, UK & Grand Rapids, Michigan, USA

First published in the UK in 2012 by Monarch Books
(a publishing imprint of Lion Hudson plc)
Wilkinson House, Jordan Hill Road, Oxford OX2 8DR, England
Tel: +44 (0)1865 302750 Fax: +44 (0)1865 302757
Email: monarch@lionhudson.com
www.lionhudson.com

ISBN 978 0 85721 023 4 (print)
ISBN 978 0 85721 265 8 (epub)
ISBN 978 0 85721 263 4 (Kindle)
ISBN 978 0 85721 266 5 (PDF)

Distributed by:
UK: Marston Book Services, PO Box 269, Abingdon, Oxon, OX14 4YN
USA: Kregel Publications, PO Box 2607, Grand Rapids, Michigan 49501

All quotations from Scripture are the author's own translation.

The text paper used in this book has been made from wood independently certified as having come from sustainable forests.

British Library Cataloguing Data
A catalogue record for this book is available from the British Library.

Printed and bound in the UK by Clays Ltd, St Ives plc.

Contents

Part 3: Scandals in Jesus' Teaching

Acknowledgments

I'd like to thank all those who have helped this book grow – in particular, John Buckeridge and Ruth Dickinson at *Christianity* magazine and Tony Collins of Lion Hudson for their encouragement; Sheron Rice for her editorial work; the team at Lion Hudson including Jenny Ward, Roger Chouler, and Simon Cox for their specialist help; and last, but by no means least, my wife, Enid, and daughters, Alice and Joanne, for their support and for keeping me "real".

Cambridge, 2011

Introduction

I work at Tyndale House, a research institute in Cambridge which specializes in biblical studies. A huge number of scholars from all over the world come here for short or long visits, so I'm forever hearing the latest discoveries and theories, and I'm surrounded by all the books and facilities I need to research them further.

Some of these coffee-break-length chapters started life as articles in *Christianity* magazine and I have added many others in a similar style. During the research and writing process I have been at different times annoyed, amazed, dismayed, delighted – and always surprised.

My personal presuppositions are that Jesus is who he claimed to be in the Gospels, and that these accounts represent what actually happened. But, of course, many people, including some of my academic colleagues, have different conclusions, so often I address more sceptical viewpoints.

To understand Jesus we have to know something about Jews of the time, and to understand the Gospels it helps a great deal if we read them with the mindset of a first-century Jew or Gentile – the people for whom they were written. My specialist area of research is early rabbinic Judaism, but this book also delves into other forms of Judaism such as that of the Dead Sea Scrolls, and into Roman and Greek culture. When we look at the Gospels through the eyes of someone from these cultures, they appear very different – problems in understanding the text are often solved and unexpected details take us unawares.

This book may challenge many traditional interpretations, but its aim is to find a foundation for historical facts about Jesus. Surprisingly, as the first chapter shows, scandals are a good place to look.

Why Look for Scandals?

Scandals are our best guarantee of historical truth in the Gospels. When disgraceful, embarrassing and shocking details about Jesus are recorded by his friends and supporters, it is much harder to disbelieve them.

Jesus was accused of being a bastard, blaspheming, abusing alcohol, partying with prostitutes, being mad and working for Satan – in other words, scandal followed him. And a huge part of his teaching and ministry tackled head-on the scandals that pervaded society and would therefore have been regarded as scandalous by his audience.

Scandals are the inconvenient truths which the Gospels could not omit without being dismissed as fiction by their first readers. If there had been no scandals, the Gospel writers wouldn't have invented them – why create potential reasons for people to dismiss Jesus? And if there *were* scandals, the original readers would remember, so the Gospel writers had to mention them and make a reply.

These scandals supply inadvertent confirmation for Christian claims. The fact that Jesus was charged with blasphemy indicates that he did claim divinity. The fact that he was stigmatized as illegitimate gives at least some credence to the stories of a miraculous birth – though sceptics would say it was a reason for inventing such stories. The fact that he spent time with prostitutes and gangsters indicates that he really did teach that *anyone* could have their life transformed. And the fact that he was charged with doing miracles by Satan's power demonstrates that even his enemies believed his miracles were real.

The Gospels are a model of how *not* to win friends and influence people. Their primary audience consisted of Jews and those Gentiles who were friends of Jews, because most of the early converts came from these groups. And yet the Gospels regularly include criticisms of Jewish leaders and generally accepted Jewish beliefs and attitudes. From the financial scams of the Temple to the belief that God rejects all disabled people and that illness is due to sin, Jesus spoke against many Jewish teachings and practices in embarrassingly public ways.

The Romans, too, didn't escape Jesus' caustic tongue. Their practice of using child slaves as sex toys enraged him: he said their punishment would be worse than undergoing a mafia-style drowning wearing concrete boots. We can contrast this with the historian Josephus' multi-volume record of the Jewish–Roman wars. Written at about the same time as the Gospels, it included only mild criticisms of Roman culture.

As well as scandals that were taking place within society, other scandals are found within Jesus' teaching itself when he said things that no one wanted to hear. He spoke more about eternal hell and coming judgment than about the popular subject of God's love – though he was also outspoken about this. The Gospel writers didn't try to help his image by editing what Jesus said, but included equally both the things that made him unpopular and popular.

When Jesus healed the sick, for example, no one complained. But when he did it on the Sabbath, or said that someone's sickness wasn't due to sin, he outraged almost everyone. The scandal attached to it highlights that it was an important aspect of Jesus' teaching. And what was scandalous in those days may simply be normal today. Letting women attend religious teaching, for example, is not scandalous in most cultures today, but in the first century, admitting that Jesus let this happen was detrimental to his standing as a religious teacher. In recognizing this kind of historical perspective, we can better understand the emphasis of Jesus' teaching.

Even the early church and the disciples themselves are presented in a scandalous way in the Gospels. Jesus had to teach his followers not to hate each other, but he also had to tell them how to forgive each other and set things straight when they did hate each other. His disciples are no superheroes; rather, they are portrayed as a motley bunch of idiots who persistently misunderstand Jesus and generally get in the way. But that's what real life is like and it shows that the Gospels are concerned with portraying reality, not fiction.

Scandals are memorable. You remember an outrageous story because everyone talks about it and you've probably passed it on to someone else yourself. When people nod, they are listening to you; when they shake their heads in disagreement they become more attentive; but when they are scandalized by something they memorize the details so that they can tell their friends about it!

Historians love scandals almost as much as newspapers do. When assessing whether an account is likely to be accurate they use terms like "criterion of embarrassment" (i.e. the more embarrassing it is for the person who records it, the more likely it is to be true) and "counter-cultural ethics" (i.e. if the subject's behaviour has been criticized by everyone else, then they are unlikely to have made it up). Of course scandals are biased, but scholars recognize that all records of history are biased and, at least with a scandal, the bias is out in the open.

Scholars are right to be sceptical. The early church must have been tempted to portray Jesus in the best possible light, and we have to assume that this is what they tried to do, just as we still do. This is what makes the scandals in the Gospels so valuable. The Gospels have been subjected to more scrutiny than any other ancient documents – and rightly so, because people don't base their lives on Caesar's *Gallic Wars* or the Dead Sea Scrolls. The life of Jesus is incomparable, so we need to know if the records are accurate.

Whole libraries have been written on the Gospels – I know, because I work in a library containing nothing but books in the realm of biblical study. I've distilled some of the most surprising and controversial scandals uncovered by scholarship so that you can judge for yourself about the real history and teaching of Jesus. The kinds of accusation made against Jesus are sometimes confirmed by sources from the same time as the Bible, so I have often highlighted evidence from the history and culture of the time. For example, we'll find that some historians have identified part of the original court records for Jesus' trial, and see that some of Jesus' teaching on subjects as varied as hell and harmonious living is paralleled in the Dead Sea Scrolls.

The chapters in this book can be read in any order; each one is self-contained and is short enough to read in a coffee break. They are also designed to be turned into talks – just add your own opening illustration and use your own words. At the end of each chapter I try to highlight something of particular relevance so that each one can be used as a discussion starter or a provocative short talk – you can perhaps change or omit this "thought" to suit your audience. And when something you read particularly surprises you, why not store it up in your head to produce in a quiet conversational moment with friends? It is sure to get a good discussion going.

I'm an academic, so I'm frequently sceptical, but I also know Jesus for myself. So the Gospels are precious to me – especially the scandal of the cross.

PART 1

SCANDALS IN JESUS' LIFE

Illegitimate Birth

My father added his mother's family name to his own, in order to make a more impressive surname. He was a barrister who needed more work and he hoped to attract a better sort of client. The ploy didn't work… and it made me the butt of endless jokes at school. Over half a century ago, when my father did this, it was a relatively novel idea. Today, it is much more common to meet someone whose name includes their mother's surname, so my children don't suffer the derision of their classmates as I did. But when the people of Nazareth called Jesus "son of Mary", the whispered sneers would have been deafening. His detractors gave him this name when he dared to preach at the synagogue in his home village. It's not until we take a look at the social background that we can recognize how great an insult this was.

Jews in the time of Jesus took their father's name as their surname. Matthew's list of disciples includes "James son of Zebedee" and "James son of Alphaeus" (see Matthew 10:2–4). In Aramaic, the Jewish language of the time, this would have been "James bar Zebedee" and "James bar Alphaeus", just like "Simon bar Jonah" (Matthew 16:17). This is the pattern found in all Jewish literature of that period and, like our surnames, they kept these names even after their father had died. For common names like "Simon" they sometimes used other naming strategies; so Simon son of Jonah also has a nickname (Peter, i.e. "Rocky"), while other Simons are named after a former affiliation ("the Zealot"), a former affliction ("the leper"), or his home town ("of Cyrene" – Matthew 10:2, 4; 26:6; 27:32). Significantly, there are no other instances in ancient literature of a Jew who was named, like Jesus, after his mother.

In Nazareth, everyone knew the scandal of Jesus' birth – it occurred less than nine months after his parents' marriage and everyone could count. In fact, after spending three months at Elizabeth's house (Luke 1:56) and other delays, Mary probably had a visible bump on her wedding day. It would have been slightly more socially acceptable if Joseph had been the father, but he denied this. So when Jesus had the temerity to preach in his home village, the gossiping turned into public outrage: "Isn't this the carpenter, the son of Mary, the brother of James, Joseph, Judas and Simon, and aren't his sisters here?" (Mark 6:3). This tirade is all the more damning because of who it leaves out – Jesus' father! It was outrageously insulting to identify him in this way and list all these family members without naming his father. Even if the subject's father had died, he would have been named – in fact it would have been even more important to name him because his eldest son should carry his name forward for posterity. This glaring omission proclaimed the scandalous fact loudly and clearly: no one knew who Jesus' father was.

While only Mark records the insult at Nazareth, the other Gospels do not ignore this scandal, and each one responds to it in a different way, reflecting their own style and perspective. Mark reads like a tabloid newspaper with its short sentences, immediacy, and friendly naivety; Matthew, like *The Times*, is concerned about political and religious establishments and seeks to highlight corruption and hypocrisy; Luke is similar to the *Guardian* – more interested in social concerns and the disadvantaged such as lepers, women and the poor; and the Gospel of John is like a more thoughtful weekly digest, such as *Newsweek* or *Time* magazine, because it was written after a considerable time of theological reflection.

Any good salesman will tell you that the best way to deal with a weakness is to address it head on, and that's what Matthew and Luke do when they give extended details about Jesus' special parentage. Matthew starts his Gospel with the genealogy of Jesus from Adam, through David, down to Joseph. Then he presents the surprise: Jesus was not the son of Joseph but of the Holy Spirit. Being concerned about the establishment, Matthew emphasizes the roles of a regal star and Eastern emissaries, and the malevolent interest paid by King Herod. Luke has a similar emphasis on the virgin birth, but starts by depicting the piety of Mary and her relative Elizabeth, the elderly priest's wife whom Mary travels to visit as soon as she falls pregnant. The unspoken implication is that Mary would not have confided in Elizabeth if she had anything to be ashamed of.

In our present society it is easy to forget how utterly unacceptable it used to be to have any sexual scandal in your parentage, but in many cultures a slur on your parentage is still the worst insult imaginable. When the Americans first tried to combat Saddam Hussein's army they had a seemingly insurmountable problem: they couldn't find it! The Iraqis had prepared vast warrens of underground bunkers over a huge area and even after several weeks of bombing the US had failed to kill or even dislodge significant numbers. Then someone who knew the Iraqi culture came up with a brilliant and successful ruse. The Americans fitted loudspeakers on armoured cars that were filled with snipers. Then they drove across the apparently empty desert broadcasting in Arabic: "Your mothers were born illegitimately." This was so unbearable for the Iraqi soldiers that they poured out of their hidden bunkers firing wildly at the loudspeakers... and becoming sitting targets for the snipers.

Jesus must have constantly faced slurs about his parentage, though these were probably rarely spoken out loud. In John's

Gospel we find a heckler who tried to disrupt Jesus' preaching by shouting out what the gossips were saying privately. Jesus had just claimed to come from his Father in heaven (John 8:18), so the heckler called out, "Where is your father?" (v. 19). While some in the crowd were asking, "What does he mean?", others were no doubt passing on the juicy details. At first Jesus ignored the interruption and continued to teach about his origins from above (vv. 21–23), but when he proclaimed that those who rejected him would die in their sins (v. 24), the heckler demanded: "Who are you?" – that is, "What's your name?" He probably hoped for an answer like, "Jesus son of Joseph" so that he could dispute it, but instead, a little later, Jesus evaded this by calling himself "The Son of Man" (v. 28). Shortly after this the heckler said: "Well, we are sons of Abraham" (i.e. good Jews), so Jesus retorted, "If you were really Abraham's sons, you wouldn't be trying to kill me" (vv. 33–40). Now the gloves were off and the heckler delivered the final blow: "At least we aren't born out of fornication!" (v. 41). You can almost hear the collective sharp intake of breath, but no one spoke up to contradict this charge.

This kind of rumour about Jesus' birth continued for hundreds of years in rabbinic literature where Jesus is called "son of Pandera". This title must date back to at least the end of the first century because rabbis in the second century were already unsure who this Pandera was. They concluded from the negative tone that the name Pandera referred to an illicit lover, who was perhaps a Roman soldier.[1]

So how does history view the scandal of Jesus' parentage? After his death and resurrection, the Jews were understandably sceptical about explanations in the Gospels that Jesus' Father was God himself, and historians are equally sceptical – though, as we'll see below, the facts about this scandal actually help to make the miracle more likely.

The job of historians is to question the motivation and accuracy of ancient reports and to decide, on the basis of other facts and their knowledge of human psychology, what actually happened. So, for example, when historians read Suetonius' report that several miracles and signs accompanied the birth of Emperor Augustus,[2] they have to decide whether this was over-enthusiastic hype or overt propaganda. And when they investigate the birth of Jesus we wouldn't expect them to use different criteria. Historical method can never easily accept a miracle because by any criteria of what is likely to have happened, a miracle will always be at the bottom of the list. Miracles are, by their nature, special, so they are never likely.

However, there are significant reasons why it is also unlikely that Joseph and Mary would have invented such a strange cover story. First, first-century Palestine was a relatively well-educated and sophisticated society, and the religious leaders of the time were particularly sceptical about improbable and unprecedented miracles. Most Jews would have regarded the story of a virgin birth as unbelievable at best and blasphemous at worst. Second, Joseph and Mary would have attracted less criticism if they'd said the child was the result of rape by a Roman soldier or pre-marital love-making. And if Joseph was a character who was brave enough to marry this apparently fallen woman, it makes sense that he would also have the courage to tell the truth. And why would they invent such a dubious story when, as the incidental references in the Gospels of John and Mark demonstrate, these claims about Jesus' birth being miraculous were simply disbelieved by most Jews? They didn't believe it in his home village or in the rest of the country, as anyone knowing that society could have predicted.

Historians have a problem: they have to choose between two equally unlikely scenarios. Either a group of religious

Jews adamantly proclaimed an extremely naive and potentially blasphemous story, or there was a miraculous birth. This is an uncomfortable choice, except for those who do not rule out the miraculous.

For all Christians, the fact that Jesus was the brunt of the gossips is a precious insight into his suffering. Isaiah predicted that the Messiah would be despised and rejected, sorrowful and grieving, afflicted with illness, wounds and punishments so severe that people would assume that he was being smitten by God (Isaiah 53:3–5). The question of his parentage was a scandal which he bore with all those who are falsely branded with moral disapproval for something outside their control – those who don't know their parents, rape victims, and those whose sexuality is damaged by child abuse. The scandal of Jesus' illegitimacy demonstrates that when God became human, he shared all our suffering and redeemed every aspect of our fallen humanity so that he could represent and redeem everyone.

Notes

1. See Joseph Klausner, *Jesus of Nazareth: His life, times and teaching*, trans. Herbert Danby, Allen & Unwin, 1925, pp. 18–45.
2. Suetonius, *Lives of the Caesars, Augustus* 94.

Ineligible Bachelor

The day my first child was born I realized that getting married hadn't changed my life much at all, in comparison! Her arrival started a completely new adventure full of excitement, fear, happiness, agonizing, fun, worry, relief, and enjoyment. For some, the prospect of marriage and/or children is not so attractive and they choose to remain single and childless, while for others this is a sad burden rather than a lifestyle choice. But for Jesus, singleness was a scandal.

Jesus' singleness, in first-century Palestine, represented profound impiety and hinted at a well-known scandal in his life. For a Jew of that time the highest ideal was to obey God, and all Jews at every level of society were aware of God's commands in Scripture. And it wasn't just the ten given at Mount Sinai; the Jews eventually counted 613 commandments in Scripture. The very first was given to Adam – "Go forth and multiply" – and every male Jew attempted to obey it. And it was pretty obvious to your family and neighbours whether or not you were obeying this commandment!

In the ancient Jewish literature of the time we can read about hundreds of individuals, but there is only one instance of an unmarried man – a studious rabbi named Simeon ben Azzi. He said that he was married to the Bible, so he didn't have time for a wife! Actually, he was probably a widower, but his friends still urged him to remarry because singleness was so unacceptable.

Girls were mostly married by the age of twelve, and if a man wasn't married by the age of twenty the gossips started comparing notes and looking for a reason.[1] Girls were married early because when they reached the age of twelve and a half they became entitled to refuse the husband their parents had arranged for them. Men had a little longer to make up their minds about who they would marry, but people soon grew suspicious. For example, although a single man was allowed to teach school children, he had to be constantly chaperoned. And if he was still single in his twenties, it was assumed there was something terribly wrong with him. Singleness was so rare and despised that no one willingly accepted this state.

So why was Jesus still single at the age of thirty? It was clear to all who knew him. No one would let his daughter marry someone of questionable parentage since, if there was any irregularity in their birth, it could cast doubt on the legitimacy of their children for ten generations. And Jesus' birth, as everyone knew, was very irregular. For one thing, it occurred too soon after his parents' wedding, and for another Joseph admitted that he wasn't the father. Most people would have regarded the story of angels and a virgin birth as a pathetic attempt to cover up the obvious – that Jesus was conceived illegitimately.

The legal term in British law for someone of illegitimate birth is "bastard". The fact that we don't use this term in polite conversation indicates the stigma which accompanied it until very recently. In Jewish society the equivalent term was a *mamzer*. There weren't many *mamzerim* (the plural of *mamzer*), partly because there was little sexual immorality in Jewish society and partly because of social pressure: they couldn't attend the Temple, and they couldn't marry anyone of legitimate birth. A *mamzer* was still obliged to get married, but they could only marry another *mamzer*.

Jesus was not a *mamzer* – at least, not officially. The Pharisees ruled that in cases of illegitimacy there had to be two witnesses to the intercourse and at Jesus' conception there were none (except perhaps for an angel!). Also, Jesus' birth did at least take place after a marriage, even if Joseph denied being the father. Jesus was therefore an "unofficial" *mamzer*. This meant that no one could stop him entering the Temple or doing other things forbidden to *mamzerim*, though no good Jewish father would ever let his daughter marry him.

I have half-jokingly warned my two teenage daughters that any boyfriend they bring home will not be good enough for me. And yet, if they brought home a drug-crazed, convicted axe murderer, I would be more likely to welcome him than a first-century Jewish father would have been to welcome Jesus as a son-in-law. Marriage to him would have brought scandal on the whole family.

Jesus not only shared the stigma of being single – he also tried to do something to alleviate it for other single people. Jewish law excused eunuchs from the command to marry, because they couldn't physically fulfil the duty to have children. Eunuchs were classified into two groups – those who were born as eunuchs (i.e. "made eunuchs by God") and those who had become eunuchs "by man" (e.g. by an injury). Jesus introduced a third category, pointing out that God did *not* require everyone to get married and attempt to have children. He said that one could *choose* voluntarily to live like a eunuch for the sake of the Kingdom (Matthew 19:12). He didn't mean that someone should castrate himself in order to be a better Christian (the third-century church leader, Origen, unfortunately did think this and castrated himself, though later in life he realized that he had misinterpreted Jesus' teaching!). Jesus meant that we could decide to serve the Kingdom of God by being single instead of getting married. There was therefore nothing impious or second-rate about being single.

Was Paul married? It is unthinkable that an obedient disciple of Gamaliel (as Paul claimed to have been in Acts 22:3) would have ignored the obligation to marry. Paul knew that disciples learned from the example of their masters, which is why he said: "Follow my example, as I follow the example of Christ" (1 Corinthians 11:1). Paul's master Gamaliel was married and had children, and yet Paul was clearly unmarried when he wrote 1 Corinthians (see 1 Corinthians 7:8). It is likely that he was widowed rather than never married. Or perhaps he was still very young when he became a Christian and he decided to be a "eunuch for the sake of the Kingdom". He certainly considered that being unmarried has some advantages for those who want to be unhampered by looking after a family (see 1 Corinthians 7:26–27, 32–35), though he assumed that most people would marry (1 Corinthians 7:7–9).

Jesus' introduction of a third group of eunuchs – those who volunteered to remain single – showed that the law to "go and multiply" didn't apply to everyone because singleness could be just as beneficial for the Kingdom. Today single people play important roles in churches and Christian organizations, but in first-century Judaism, singleness was potentially scandalous and a bar from any leadership. Paradoxically, some churches today still tend to stigmatize singleness by focussing on marriage and children.

Living in a world where "virgin" is an abusive or comic label can be a heavy burden for many single Christians. For most of them, of course, the stigma is far less of an issue than the desire for the love and intimacy of a marriage. Jesus suffered alongside them as a single person every day. Admired by many for his teaching and miracles, he also faced the whispers which kept spreading the scandal of his irregular birth. It was a stigma he embraced in order to suffer with us and bring all of humanity back to God.

Notes

1.   Mishnah Niddah 5.6–8; Babylonian Talmud Qiddushin 29b.

Fraudulent Miracles

A week after a service of prayer for healing at my church, an elderly lady came forward to testify. She came to the front beaming and boomed into the microphone as though she didn't really trust it to work: "My piles are completely healed!" Then she started telling us many more details than we wanted to know! Eventually I wrested the microphone from her as politely as I could. We gave thanks for her healing, though my reaction to the unsavoury details made me realize that one reason why many might think that the age of healing miracles is over is that often we simply don't talk about them. We don't tell our doctor that our church is praying for us and we are embarrassed to tell work colleagues that we are praying for solutions to problems. As a result, when our prayer is answered, it seems false to talk about it.

In the Bible, amazing miracles seem to happen all the time – that is, until you count them all and divide by a few thousand years. The only person in the Bible whose life really is full of wonderful miracles is Jesus. More instances of healing are recorded during his three-year ministry than in the rest of the Bible added together, and some of those included large groups of ill people.[1] It would be understandable to think that the Gospel writers reported Jesus' miracles so often because they gave him such credibility and were something that people really wanted to hear about. In fact, quite the opposite was true.

Healing miracles were a frequent source of scandal in the first century – in fact the whole subject of miracles was viewed with distaste. They were regarded as scams that were carried out on the gullible – a way to start a new religion and get rich quick. Oenomaus and Lucian, Greek writers and philosophers in the second century, wrote some telling exposés of so-called "miracles". They discovered, for example, that the phenomenon of one religion's "talking statues" was nothing more than cleverly concealed speaking tubes. When Josephus rewrote the Old Testament for first-century Roman readers (his *Antiquities of the Jews*), he omitted most of the healing miracles because his readers wouldn't think them genuine. Belief in miracle-workers was out of fashion – too many charlatans had claimed fake "wonders" to promote themselves.

Jews, too, were embarrassed about miracles. When the first-century Jewish writer Philo commented on the Old Testament for Jewish readers, he interpreted miracles "philosophically" – that is, as non-literal events. But most Jews were even less accepting: Jesus' enemies accused him of doing miracles by the power of the devil, a reflection of how low their opinion of the miraculous had sunk. Jewish political rulers (mainly Sadducees) didn't believe in anything supernatural, whereas the religious leaders (mainly Pharisees) did believe in miracles, though only in theory – they relegated them to the "good old days" of Old Testament times, hundreds of years previously.

Over the next five centuries, miracles gradually came back into favour; people began to accept them – or became more easy to fool again, depending on your viewpoint.[2] Stories about miracles performed by a small number of rabbis in Jesus' time were recorded by Jews in later centuries. Two of them, Honi and Hanina, were particularly renowned for their miracles, though the description of their feats in earlier records is not so extraordinary: Honi had his prayers for rain answered once, and Hanina's prayers for the sick were answered occasionally.[3] Neither man was respected much by rabbis of his own generation.[4]

At that time, therefore, miracles would not have helped Jesus gain much acceptance among the Jews – rather the reverse – and perhaps this is why he was so coy about them.

It is also why Jesus didn't use miracles to authenticate his ministry, like Elijah and Moses did. Elijah called the nation together to see his fire from heaven at Mount Carmel and Moses very publicly made his staff into a snake and later used it to part the Red Sea. In contrast, Jesus told those whom he had healed to "say nothing". Most miracles were done in secret, among small groups or in someone's home, after the crowds had gone (for example, Matthew 8:14–16). In fact, the pattern suggests that Jesus carried out many other healings in private with the story never getting out.

Even when Jesus fed the thousands, it was unostentatious. In one sense there was nothing particularly "extraordinary" about it; he didn't make a mountain of food – it was simply that the food didn't run out. The miracle which stands out because of its very different circumstances is the raising of Lazarus: it was witnessed by a large crowd and, unlike almost all of Jesus' other miracles, it took place near a city. The reaction to it was probably what Jesus expected: his enemies started plotting to kill him (John 11:46–50).

The reason the Gospels give for Jesus' miracles is his "compassion". This is a rather sanitized translation of an unusual Greek word (*splagchnizomai*), which can best be understood literally by the modern term "gut-wrenching". It was the only word the writers could find to describe Jesus' extreme reaction to human suffering. He was so overwhelmed when he saw illness, hunger and demonic fear that he just had to do something, even if it put him in danger.

The first Christian teachers, the early Church Fathers,

continued to keep quiet about Jesus' miracles because of the scandal attached to them. They concentrated instead on his ethics and self-sacrifice because these were much more likely to impress non-believers at that time. Justin Martyr did refer to Gospel healings in the early second century, but only to answer the claim that the god Asclepius healed as many illnesses as Jesus.[5]

The popular cult of Asclepius was an exception to the prevailing opinion – it was a healing religion which was respectable. Pilgrims would visit the temples of Asclepius and spend the night there after ritual purification and making sacrifices. Many miracles were claimed, though statisticians would be unimpressed. The few who were healed were asked to provide monuments to celebrate it, so that successes were highlighted. But failures were hidden: no records were kept of those who weren't healed, and anyone likely to die was expelled because the sanctuary was supposedly "defiled" by death – which certainly cut down the apparent failure rate!

Modern medical trials normally compare a new treatment with a placebo (for example, an injection of water or a pill without any medical ingredients). A placebo generally has 20 per cent of the effectiveness of the actual treatment. Such trials demonstrate that the power of suggestion or expectation has a remarkable effect on the ability of the human body to repair itself. In the first century, spending a night at a temple would produce a very strong expectation, so we would expect a proportion of those who did so to be healed.

Jesus' miracles, however, were undeniable, even by his enemies. They found them so impossible to refute that they resorted to attributing them to the devil – including (absurdly) his exorcisms (Matthew 12:24–26)! In the Jewish records of Jesus' trial, which have been preserved in ancient texts (see the chapter "Censored Arrest Warrant"), Jesus was charged with "sorcery".

This charge implied that the Jews believed Jesus' miracles were real because they distinguished between "magic", which they realized was just a matter of trickery, and "sorcery", which they reserved for real miracles performed through demonic powers.[6]

Jesus was totally unlike ancient or modern healing gurus who loudly announce their few successes; he tried to shun the limelight and there are no suggestions that he was ever unsuccessful in healing someone. He didn't demand anything from the person being healed. He didn't demand incredible faith – even the tiniest mustard-seed amount was enough. He didn't demand purity – he forgave sins first, if that was a problem (Mark 2:1). The only criterion mentioned in the Gospels was that he healed out of "compassion" – he loved people so much that he couldn't bear to see them suffer.

Miracles still happened after Jesus' time on earth, but only occasionally. We have no record of anyone still being ill after they had come to Jesus for healing, but it was different after his ascension. Although there were still wonderful miracles, they didn't take place all, or even most, of the time. When early Christians were ill or injured, they prayed for healing, but they didn't assume it would definitely happen – they knew that a miracle was a rare event. For example, when Eutychus fell out of a window and was picked up dead, the onlookers were wonderfully surprised by the miracle Paul carried out in restoring him (Acts 20:9–10). And when Epaphroditus was ill there was no instantaneous cure. His home church and Paul were extremely saddened, but were later able to rejoice when, by God's mercy, Epaphroditus recovered (Philippians 2:25–27). When Paul himself was ill – probably with eye problems, the worst possible illness for a scholar! – he kept praying and praying without being healed (2 Corinthians 12:7–9; Galatians 4:15).

Today there are still miracles. In fact, because they are spread all over the world, there are more miracles done in Jesus' name than he ever did himself while on earth. But my impression is that genuine miracles tend to occur "off-stage". When televangelists famed for their healing miracles are asked to produce medical records in proof, they suddenly become concerned about confidentiality and say the records aren't available. But the sick who are prayed for by small church groups frequently do confound medical expectations without courting publicity.

Does God pick and choose whom to heal? Why are more healings reported in developing countries? Is it because the need is greater or because more people are taken in by fake miracle-workers? Do some churches experience more miracles because they pray more or because they see what they expect to see? It is as easy to be sceptical today as it was in Jesus' day, but even the most disbelieving in the first century were unable to deny that Jesus' miracles were real. Sometimes scepticism is based on little more than a failure to investigate the facts.

Notes

1. See 34 miracles of Jesus at http://en.wikipedia.org/wiki/Miracles_attributed_to_Jesus
2. See Eric Eve, *The Healer from Nazareth: Jesus' miracles in historical context*, SPCK, 2009, pp. 40–46.
3. Mishnah Taanit 3.8; Tosepheta Berakhot 2.30.
4. See Eve, *The Healer from Nazareth*, pp. 6–25.
5. Justin, *Apology* 22.6.
6. Mishnah Sanhedrin 7.10.

Bad Table Manners

My mother said that good manners are a sign of respect for others. They are supposed to minimize conflict because they are rules which everyone follows without needing to be reminded. But sometimes they become a battle zone, as all parents know.

Our waiter at a posh London club used rules as his weapons. I was extremely hot – we'd walked hurriedly to arrive in time for an evening meal – so I hung my jacket over my chair to cool off. Up stepped the waiter: "Excuse me, sir, but jackets must be worn for dinner." I duly complied and then tried ordering a meal: "As it says on the menu, sir, no cooked meals can be ordered after 9 p.m. But you may order a cold sandwich." My watch said 9:02 p.m., but the waiter wouldn't budge from the written rule. Then an Australian in our group took up the challenge: "Well, there's no rule on the menu about breakfast times, so I'd like to order a cooked breakfast." The rest of us looked at each other. British manners weren't getting us very far. Without speaking we came to a unanimous decision: we would follow "Australian rules". The defeated waiter reluctantly went off, no doubt to tell the kitchen staff about his uncouth customers.

The Jewish religion has lots of rules about eating and table manners. My favourite is the rule that forbids reading books at mealtimes. The reason is not that it is rude or distracting, but that bookworms (tiny larvae which eat paper) may fall out into the food. This is bad because bookworms aren't kosher!

The Jews of Jesus' day had to follow a mountain of rules about table manners and sometimes these created anything but harmony. We have records of some of the disagreements about the exact details. For example, everyone agreed that at the end of a meal, the head of the group would say a final prayer of Thanksgiving for it over a full goblet of wine. Three things had to happen before this blessing: wiping crumbs off the table; pouring the wine; and washing hands. But there were disputes about the order in which these should happen. Hillelite Pharisees said it should begin with pouring, then washing, and finally wiping; but Shammaite Pharisees set down the order as wiping, washing, and then pouring the wine. This disagreement was very serious because accidentally eating crumbs could theoretically make one liable to the death penalty!

Before you dismiss all ancient Jews as crazy, I'd better explain. The Old Testament law stipulated that a tenth of all food must be given to the tribe of Levi, so that they could spend their time on religious tasks instead of farming. The priests (who were part of that tribe) got a tenth of that tenth (i.e. a hundredth) – a portion that should never be eaten by anyone who was not a priest, on pain of death.

Food was normally tithed by the farmers, but a good market-stall owner would tithe it again just in case, and good cooks tithed it yet again, just to be certain. However, the Pharisees wanted to make absolutely sure that they never ate the priests' portion even by accident, so if they weren't completely sure that the food had been tithed, they removed a hundredth of what was on their plate before eating any. They cut off a tiny piece and threw it in the fire or crumbled it up to make sure that no one ate it. (If a priest was sitting at the table, they might have given it to him, though I doubt that he'd have wanted it.) As a result of this practice, even some of the crumbs on the table might be deadly!

Saying the Thanksgiving prayer after a meal was another complex duty for Pharisees in Jesus' day because its wording changed subtly depending on how many men were present.[1] The prayer started slightly differently when said for three men, for ten men, for a hundred men, and for a thousand men. (Women could also be present at meals, but their numbers didn't affect which prayer to use.) Before someone prayed, therefore, it was important that they counted the number of men present so that they'd know the correct words to use.

I don't suppose every home always followed all these rules when guests weren't there, any more than we always use fish knives to eat fish. But at public gatherings like weddings, the neighbours would be watching and that's when they remembered all their table manners.

We can see some of these table manners enacted in the Gospels when Jesus fed the four thousand and the five thousand. The crowds were actually bigger than this but only the men were counted (Matthew 14:21; 15:28). We might wonder why the Gospel writers didn't record how many people were there in total, as this would have been even more impressive – "Twelve thousand men, women and children", for example. But they couldn't do this because the women and children hadn't been counted. They had automatically sat down in groups of fifty and one hundred men (Mark 6:40), as was normal good manners when a large group met to eat. It made it easier for the prayer-giver to count them and know the correct wording to use for the Thanksgiving prayer.

The baskets of fragments left over from the loaves were also due to good manners. These were more than mere crumbs because a fragment (Greek *klasma*) was something that was broken off deliberately, such as a tithe. Since this quantity of tithes couldn't simply be left on the hillside, they were collected in baskets so that they could be offered to a priest (even though he would most likely burn them – well, would you want to eat them?).

If you think about it, this display of normal good manners actually implied something quite scandalous. It was saying in effect that God needed to tithe the loaves and hadn't – or, in other words, that God was impious. At a wedding feast or a banquet people didn't tithe in this way because it would have insulted the host, who should be trusted to set aside the required tithe before serving the food. The crowds were therefore insulting God by tithing this food. Even though they knew it came from him (John 6:26), they tithed it as if he couldn't be trusted!

I can imagine Jesus holding his tongue and not criticizing the people about this because they were simply doing what they'd been taught. But a short while later, when Pharisees accused Jesus' disciples of eating with unpurified hands, he spoke out with a rare display of anger: "You hypocrites – you teach human traditions as though they are the doctrines of God!" (Mark 7:6–7).

Their rules about hand-washing weren't concerned with hygiene – they were ceremonial cleansings that preceded the prayer which accompanied the meal. And the point Jesus was making was that these rules weren't found in the Old Testament, but the Pharisees taught them as if God had commanded it. It wasn't that he was against hand-washing or foot-washing *per se* – he did this himself at the last supper when he prepared to serve the others – but he *was* against the Pharisees' emphasis on rules like these because they actually distracted people from the more important aspects of following God.

Jesus finally told the Pharisees that their words were worse than faeces, though fortunately, for well-mannered church congregations, he didn't express himself quite so bluntly: he said that what comes out of our mouths can express the sin in our hearts, whereas what goes into our mouths simply comes out the other end (Mark 7:15–23).

In today's English, Jesus might have said: "You Pharisees are so far from walking the walk, you aren't even talking the talk. Nothing but bad comes out of your mouths – put-downs and petty complaints, instead of respect and encouragement." The real scandal was that they paid more attention to the superficial, man-made niceties than the words and actions that really matter to God.

My mother was right: good manners show respect for others. But there are many other, more important, ways to show God's love and concern for people and, in the end, what we say to them conveys our attitude far more effectively than our table manners. Sometimes the most hurtful and cutting remarks can be made during polite table conversation when people play the game of elevating their own standing by subtly putting others down. While we might want to make sure we use the right knife when we dine in company, we should, more importantly, make sure that we build up and encourage others rather than cutting them down.

Notes
1. This rule fell into disuse soon after Jesus' day – see the debate at Mishnah Berakhot 7.3.

Alcohol Abuse

The first funeral I took as a minister was that of a man in his early twenties. He didn't go to church and when I talked with his family, I found that he didn't go to college, to work, or even out with friends much. But one night some "mates" managed to drag him out for a drink. To get him "in the mood" they encouraged him to consume almost a whole bottle of brandy. Then they helped him home, where he slept so deeply that he didn't wake up when he was sick. He inhaled his vomit and died.

Statistically, alcohol is the most dangerous drug in the UK. It kills about 9,000 people a year through accidents, illnesses or alcohol-related violence – over four times the total for all illegal drugs put together. But alcohol does have some benefits. As a relaxant it lowers blood pressure and reduces inhibitions which stop some people from enjoying themselves. As Psalm 104:15 says, it "gladdens the heart". But almost every other reference to alcohol in the Bible is negative – from Noah's drunkenness, which led to a family split (Genesis 9:20–27), to the picture of the drunk prostitute who will rule the world in Revelation 17.

Drunkenness was at the heart of a religion which became popular in New Testament times. According to Euripides' play *The Bacchae*, it started half a millennium earlier when a strikingly handsome stranger strode into Greece with a troop of beautiful Turkish dancing girls who worshipped him as a god. Dionysus (known as Bacchus in Roman mythology) was portrayed as having androgynous features, blond curls (almost unknown to southern Europeans) and a charismatic personality which soon won admirers and followers for his new religion. Preparation for worship was easy – you got drunk – and the rites involved dancing to lively music, "prophesying" and orgies. Evidence of this worship is found everywhere the Roman civilization spread, including Palestine.

On Pentecost morning, the crowd that gathered probably thought the excited and babbling Christians were worshipping Bacchus. Peter tried to disabuse them of this, saying, "It's only 9 a.m." (Bacchus worship happened at night), "and we aren't full of wine but full of the Spirit." Peter quoted Joel, who said: "Your sons and daughters will prophesy, your old men will dream dreams" (Joel 2:28). He was pointing to one way in which Christianity and Bacchus worship *were* similar – they both promoted social cohesion by involving old and young, male and female – but Christian worship involved real prophecy and real joy, instead of the temporary highs of drunkenness.

The suspicion about drunkenness in Christianity refused to go away. It was sometimes difficult to distinguish between believers' joyful Spirit-filled worship and the rowdy singing of the inebriated (Ephesians 5:18). Orgies with excessive drinking were socially acceptable in Roman society, but scandal-mongers accused Christians of drinking the blood of babies at drunken feasts. Perhaps rumours started when someone overheard phrases like "body and blood"! The first-century Roman historian Tacitus appeared to believe all the rumours, calling Christianity a "vile and shameful" religion. It didn't help when some Christians actually did get drunk at church meals (see 1 Corinthians 11:21). This led to repeated warnings in the New Testament against drunkenness and urging self-control (Galatians 5:21–23; 1 Timothy 3:2–3; 1 Peter 4:3, 7).

Alcohol was a normal part of culture in New Testament times and many Roman meals ended with a "symposium" – a drinking party. (Here in Cambridge I attend lots of academic symposiums but so far none have involved getting intoxicated!) Many men regarded these as times for serious discussion, during which they drank as much alcohol as they could – or as much as their host could afford. Just like today, many believed that alcohol made them more witty and intelligent.

The Jewish Passover meals were in danger of ending in the same way. In everyday life the Jews' main drink was water – safe drinking water was freely available from numerous wells or could be bought cheaply from street-sellers. When they drank wine, they added water to it – a custom which is preserved in many Eucharist ceremonies. At Passover, however, wine was a compulsory part of the meal for all Jews – and some wanted to make the most of it! Originally there were only three ritual cups of wine, but many Jews wanted to end the meal with a Roman *epikômos* – a binge-drinking session. The rabbis put their foot down and instead created a closing ceremony, later called the *aphikomen*, which involved just a single (fourth) cup of wine after the meal.

When Jesus celebrated his last Passover with his disciples, he rejected this fourth cup of wine. As usual, the first cup was followed by an "appetizer" of unleavened bread with bitter herbs and the second was followed by the main supper. The third cup was traditionally drunk next, followed by the singing of Psalms, but before this cup Jesus did things differently, introducing some extra unleavened bread and instituting the Eucharist. The third "cup after supper" was then drunk and Jesus declared that he would not drink wine again till they met together in the Kingdom. The final Psalms were sung and the group went to Gethsemane (Mark 14:22–26) without drinking the fourth cup.

Why did three of the four evangelists choose to record Jesus' rejection of this last cup of wine? Perhaps it was to counter the pernicious accusations about drunkenness in the church. Jesus himself was accused of alcohol abuse – both Matthew and Luke record the claim that he was "a glutton and a drunkard" (Matthew 11:19; Luke 7:34). John meets this head on by reporting Jesus' miracle of making hundreds of gallons of water into wine! Jesus didn't deny that he went to more parties than most; instead, he replied that his accusers were being inconsistent – criticizing John the Baptist for being over-abstemious and himself for being over-indulgent.

Figures show that alcohol misuse is one of the most serious public health issues facing the UK today. It is a powerful drug which many people cannot cope with and it ruins the lives of countless individuals in every nation. In Western countries it is a common cause of violence and the third greatest cause of "lifestyle" deaths after obesity and smoking. The binge-drinking culture of our young adult population, with its careless pursuit of a few hours of "blissful" escapism, is reminiscent of the Dionysian religion of New Testament times.

One might say it would have been better if the Bible had banned alcohol but, as so often, God asks us to do something more difficult: to be responsible and self-controlled. C. S. Lewis' fictional demon Screwtape pointed out that the devil has never succeeded in creating anything evil, but has managed to corrupt many good things. Alcohol is a good example of this – a wonderful part of creation which has become one of the most dangerous recreational drugs.

The twenty-first-century church is facing the same issues with the use of alcohol as the church in the first century. I am encouraged by the way the Street Pastors initiative has responded to the problem of binge-drinking. The emptiness of lives that find escape in alcohol is, at its heart, a spiritual one. And although there is choice involved, we must not judge alcoholism as being something which is only self-inflicted. The trigger is not normally alcohol alone, but usually includes a crisis or underlying trauma combined with a specific type of metabolism that leads to dependency. For those who have a drink problem, we can point the way to practical help and support, and, above all, to Jesus, who bore all our sin and shame – including the shame of being accused of alcohol abuse.

Disruptive Worship

My father would probably have subscribed to the maxim: "Children should be seen and not heard." He died when I was ten, but I remember learning to play chess aged four or five, because it was one of the few ways I could interact with him. He was born in Hong Kong in 1905, which was behind the times like most ex-pat communities. They lived like early Victorians, dressed in starched wing collars, and treated children as insignificant until they could take part in adult activities.

In Britain, however, the late Victorians had "discovered" childhood. Authors such as Lewis Carroll celebrated children as creative and playful individuals who are important and special in their own right. We now regard childhood as a precious time when some of the most creative thinking of one's life can occur.

In Jesus' day children were also considered of little significance – best ignored until they became adults who could carry out important functions. Fortunately they achieved adulthood at a fairly young age – thirteen for boys and twelve and a half for girls. This meant that a thirteen-year-old girl could choose whom to marry, though the reaction of most parents to this fact is very revealing: they made sure their daughters were engaged by the age of twelve! The main role of children was to do the will of their parents.

Children were barely recognized as individuals. We can see a hint of this attitude in the Gospels. Matthew rarely named Jesus when he was a child, referring to him merely as "the child" eight times. Luke does the same when referring to John and Jesus –

for example, when Jesus' parents reprimanded him for staying behind in the Temple, they said: "Child, why did you do this?" (Luke 1:76; 2:48). It was normal not to refer to children by their names.

Jesus reversed this mindset completely, regarding children as almost more important than adults. In these same Gospels, Jesus says that children (in contrast to his disciples) believe in him and are humble, and are therefore model citizens of the Kingdom (Matthew 18:1–6). We normally think that Jesus was commending certain characteristics which children tend to have, but Jesus actually went much further. He implied that the Kingdom was actually *for* children and that some adults could join them if they were like them (Matthew 19:14).

The disciples, slow on the uptake as usual, expected Jesus to see children as a nuisance, like any other adult at that time. They didn't realize that he really did love the company of children. Children recognize love, and when they flocked round Jesus the disciples tried to shoo them away. But Jesus, of course, welcomed them.

Jewish children and women could not lead prayers, even at home. Women were considered inferior to men and were exempted from most prayers mandated by the law, as well as many other commandments. The rule was that they didn't have to fulfil any positive commandment which was time-limited. (A cynic might say that they were excused from anything which might prevent them feeding their husband!) Children had to obey even fewer of the commandments, perhaps because they were regarded as even less important than women. On many occasions the rabbis ruled that a specific law need not or could not be obeyed by "a deaf-dumb, an imbecile, or a child". In other words, children were discounted because they couldn't understand.

In Jewish life, the exception to the norm was the Passover meal, in which children were fully involved. Unlike the fast of the Day of Atonement or the meals of the Feast of Tabernacles, Passover *had* to be attended by women and children – and even circumcised slaves could attend. In fact, the youngest child of the house had a special role: at a key point in the ceremony he had to ask three questions which highlighted the heart of the meal's significance. It is interesting that Jesus used this meal as the model for instituting Communion (Eucharist or the Lord's Supper).

Leonardo da Vinci painted Jesus eating the Last Supper with twelve men. But where are the women and servants who cooked the meal, and where are their children? Unless Jesus stopped in the middle of the meal to throw them out, they would still have been there. I think that Jesus deliberately chose this meal so that everyone would be included.

Jesus' attitude to children is startlingly clear on Palm Sunday, when he was overjoyed to see young children leading the worship. They were chanting from Psalm 118:25–26: "*Hosanna*" ("Save us!") and "Blessed is he who comes in the name of the Lord." All the adults were joining in, but the Pharisees looked on with thunder in their eyes. They demanded that Jesus stop the children, but he replied: "If they kept quiet, the stones would shout out" (Luke 19:40). The Pharisees would have recognized this as an allusion to Psalm 118:21–22, which says the Lord "answered me" and "the stone the builders rejected has become the cornerstone." No doubt they recognized the accusation that Jesus was making – that they were the builders who rejected this popular new cornerstone.

How did the children get the crowds to join in – surely they would have been silenced all too quickly? The explanation is that they were shouting a chant. And the rule was that if anyone started a holy chant, it was impious not to join in and complete it. The rule specifically said that even a child could shout "Blessed is he" and *everyone* had to finish: "… who comes in the name of the Lord."[1]

The *hosanna* chant was used at the Feast of Tabernacles, when crowds of ordinary people spent all day circling the Great Altar in the Temple, waving palm branches and chanting, "*Ana Yehovah, hoshi'ah-na*" ("Now Lord, save us!"). The rabbis tried to limit this to one circuit of the altar because they complained that the words became slurred when chanted over and over again. They ended up chanting, "*Ani waho hosanna*", which is like starting the Lord's Prayer with "Ah Far in'evan".[2]

The chanting crowds particularly scandalized and frightened the Jewish leaders because it reminded everyone of the great Jewish hero Judas Maccabaeus who rode into Jerusalem in 165 BC after ousting Antiochus IV, who had desecrated the Temple. Judas rode into the city "with praise and palm branches", and then went to purify the Temple.[3] These same chants were used every year at the festival of Hanukkah, which commemorated this event. So, when Jesus deliberately chose to ride into Jerusalem on his way to the Temple, the crowds couldn't have missed this parallel.

This was dangerous, because the Romans were sure to find out and interpret it as a military threat. The Pharisees tried to calm things, but they couldn't control the children, and the children were egging on the crowds. What brilliant fun – making the adults chant and chant! How the children must have loved it! And Jesus was letting them continue as long as they liked, while the Pharisees looked over their shoulders and worried about the consequences.

Did the church follow Jesus' example and allow children to lead worship? No. Did they let children share in Communion?

Maybe. The early church celebrated Communion after a common meal called an Agape Feast (a "Love Meal"). Presumably whole families attended, as at Passover meals, so children would have been present. But did they take Communion or just receive a "blessing", as in many churches today? We don't know for sure, but the fact that Communion was based on Passover – where children joined in and even had a special role – would mean that unless someone told them differently, believers would automatically assume children were to take part.

Later, of course, the church did restrict Communion only to those who could "examine themselves" (1 Corinthians 11:28). This was interpreted over time to mean only those who had been examined and passed their catechesis – a kind of oral exam conducted by a priest to make sure they believed and understood everything correctly. Within a couple of centuries, the common meals had been dropped and Communion became a complex rite carried out only by qualified priests and shared only with qualified believers. Children were once again excluded and put in their place, having to wait until they were adult before they could join in properly.

Some churches still operate with what we might call an old-fashioned attitude to children: it is important to teach them, but there is nothing an adult can learn from them; children are allowed "do something" in church to entertain adults, but their main role is to learn and to wait. Many churches, however, do recognize the valuable contribution children can make and celebrate their creativity, but even then some still refuse to recognize their children as fully Christian. Only when they are old enough and can understand enough theology, can they take Communion.

When I see children excluded from taking Communion, I often find myself wondering what Jesus thinks of it. His attitude to children was revolutionary – even the disciples were scandalized by it. He was in constant demand, yet he stopped to spend time with children. Jesus loved to be with those who loved him – and I'm sure he'd welcome even the smallest and least educated child to his table.

Notes
1. Babylonian Talmud Sukkah 38b.
2. Mishnah Berakhot 9.5; Mishnah Sukkah 4.5; Jerusalem Talmud Sukkah 3.10, 16a. We do not know how exactly they pronounced "Yehovah".
3. 2 Maccabees 10:6–8.

Exposing Temple Scams

Terry Herbert was an unemployed metal-detector enthusiast who in 2009 stumbled on the largest hoard of Saxon gold in history in a Staffordshire field. He and the landowner shared its value – £3.3 million. The objects he found were military – mostly gold ornaments from swords and helmets – and the soldiers who owned them were probably Christians because they carried some crosses and a band of gold inscribed: "Rise up, Lord; may Your enemies be scattered." Instead, it seems likely that their enemies defeated them and then buried their gold. No doubt the conquerors meant to come back later to retrieve the treasure, but for some reason this never happened – perhaps they fought another battle in which they themselves were defeated.

Until recent centuries burying your coins or gold ornaments was a common way of protecting your property when fleeing home and often people were not able to return for it. In 1960 a hoard of money dating back to the time of Jesus was found buried on Mount Carmel. It was probably a collection of Temple tax from an outlying village that was being carried to Jerusalem because it added up to an exact number of half shekels plus the percentage charged by Temple money-changers. These people taking the villagers' payment to the Temple had presumably fallen victim to bandits but managed to hide the coins before they were killed.

Although the Temple tax in Jesus' day was the focus of several scandals, most Jews respected the Temple and paid it religiously. However, Jesus was one of the few Temple-using Jews who didn't believe it was compulsory to pay the tax, as we see from the mild reproof he gave Peter (Matthew 17:24–27). And he certainly didn't like the money-changers – he drove them out of the Temple with a whip (John 2:15). He was angry, of course, because he believed that the Temple was being desecrated; it had been turned into a noisy house of commerce rather than a "house of prayer" (Matthew 21:13). But his fury was probably also prompted by something else: the financial scandals.

One scandal was that the Temple had more money than it could use, yet it was always striving to collect even more – and by increasingly dubious means. First, the Temple authorities decided to charge the half-shekel tax annually instead of once per lifetime as the law of Moses decreed (Exodus 30:12–15). With an average lifespan of 30 years, this meant that they were over-charging by about 3,000 per cent. To make this scandal complete, they excused all priests from paying the tax, even though the law of Moses levied it on everyone.[1]

When people came to pay their tax they were then faced with another charge, because the Temple demanded payment in the relatively rare half-shekel coins that were made in Tyre. This meant that everyone had to exchange their shekels with the money-changers who were licensed to work inside the Temple. They only charged 4 per cent,[2] which is roughly what an airport foreign exchange bureau charges today, but it was, nonetheless, a compulsory extra – and no doubt the Temple got a cut of the profits.

The second scandal concerned the type of coins the tax had to be paid in – the half-shekels. The priests didn't demand these particular coins for religious reasons, but for financial ones – the half-shekels made in Tyre had a higher silver concentration than shekels made elsewhere. But there was also a problem with them: the shekels of Tyre were decorated with the head of Melqarth –

that is, Tyre's version of the god Baal!

The Temple authorities were scandalously demanding coins that bore an image of Baal, simply to gain a slight financial advantage! When the Pharisees realized Jesus was against the Temple tax, they tried to catch him out with a question about taxes to Caesar. Jesus asked them for a coin and someone handed him a denarius with an image of Caesar on it. Jesus asked, "Whose image is on this coin?" Jesus won the argument by saying: "Give to Caesar what is Caesar's and to God what is God's." The Temple authorities must have let out a sigh of relief when they saw it was a denarius. Think how much worse it could have been if he'd been given one of the special half-shekels which the Temple insisted on, with an image of Baal on it. Jesus could have condemned them for demanding offerings not for Jehovah but for Baal!

These scandals were acknowledged by others but only Jesus stuck his neck out and criticized the authorities publicly. There were also many other minor scams, such as selling surplus offerings,[3] or ordering offerings ahead at one price and then using the Temple's financial clout to make a profit: when the price went up, they insisted on paying for them at the original lower price; when it went down they insisted on paying at the new price.[4]

The biggest scandal is found in a question which comes up occasionally in rabbinic writings: what happened to all the left-over money? It is estimated that the Temple collected more than a million shekels per year, which was enough to pay the wages of three Roman legions.[5] And yet the priests weren't paid anything – they went home with no more than bits of food offerings. Where did all this money go?

The money was supposed to pay for the public sacrifices (the morning and evening offerings, and festival offerings such as the lamb of atonement). Everyone wanted their coins to contribute to this, as it made them feel that their money was received by God himself. However, only a proportion of the total received – nine baskets of coins – was needed to pay for these offerings, so the priests picked out the actual coins used by a form of lottery. Three times a year (probably at the three major festivals) a priest dipped a basket three times into the mountain of collected coins to extract those to be used to purchase offerings. Gamaliel (the rabbi who taught Paul) was said to have a special technique for making sure his coin went into that basket. He used to wait for the priest to come, then throw his coin onto the pile just in front of the basket where it would get scooped up.

We have no idea what happened to the rest of the money. Just after the Temple was destroyed, the rabbis debated this and finally concluded that the priests had kept adding thicker and thicker gold plate to the inside walls of the Temple where no one could see it. In other words, they found a good explanation to justify where the money went. How naive! We know that the high priest lived in relative luxury (archaeologists found Caiaphas' family home in 1990) and the ruling Sadducees were famous for using nothing but silver and gold for their meal-time place settings. Sadducees believed that there was no life after death, so they made a virtue of living as luxuriously as possible in this life.[6] Nevertheless, it is difficult to imagine how any amount of luxury could expend these millions of shekels. What they were doing with the missing millions remains a mystery.

The New Testament is full of warnings about the love of money: it is "a root of all kinds of evil" (1 Timothy 6:10); it was the motive for Judas' betrayal of Jesus (according to John 12:4–6); and it led Ananias and Sapphira to lie about the proportion of their giving, which to everyone's astonishment God punished by death (Acts 5:1–6). None of these passages criticized wealth itself, and neither did Jesus. While he demanded that the rich ruler give away all of his wealth, Jesus also praised Zacchaeus when he offered to give away only half of his wealth (Luke 18:22–24; 19:8–9). The difference, we assume, is that Zacchaeus was no longer in love with wealth – as indicated by his offer to give it away without any prompting.

Money can conquer us, if we hold it too tightly. The millions of coins which the Sadducees scandalously manoeuvred into the Temple funds eventually fell into the hands of their conquerors, the Romans. In modern times it seems as though there is a new financial scandal almost every day; theft and fraud are prevalent among both the rich and the poor. Though the majority of churches carefully steward the money that they are given, sadly, there are parts of the church that act without integrity – the financial scandals of some TV evangelists are the most obvious examples. Jesus' story about the farmer who amassed great riches but died on the day of his retirement is still an important warning for us today. Treasure in heaven is still a better investment than treasure on earth.

Notes

1. Mishnah Sheqalim 1.3.
2. Mishnah Sheqalim 1.7 – though one rabbi thought they charged twice this amount.
3. Mishnah Sheqalim 4.3–4.
4. Mishnah Sheqalim 4.9.
5. This was based on the number of Passover celebrants at Tosephta Pesachim 4.15. Even if these numbers are exaggerated, we know that Antiochus Epiphanes looted the Temple in 167 BC (Josephus, *Antiquities* 12.248–50+5.4), and yet when Pompey conquered Jerusalem in 63 BC the Temple had replaced all the gold vessels and they had accumulated 6 million shekels in spare cash (Josephus, *Antiquities* 14.72+4.4).
6. *Avot de Rabbi Nathan* 5.2. Note that this was written by their rivals.

Supplanting Passover

I once gave my wife an anniversary present a day late. I remember feeling slightly apprehensive about what she would say, but to my relief she admitted that she'd forgotten too. Perhaps she was just being extra-forgiving. But the correct date for a celebration is important, and Jews in New Testament times couldn't simply decide, for the sake of convenience, to celebrate a festival on another day. That would, perhaps, be even more disrespectful than Christians celebrating the resurrection on Good Friday! And yet it appears that Jesus did exactly that when he ate his last supper with the disciples as a Passover meal.

The Synoptic Gospels (Matthew, Mark and Luke) clearly say that Jesus celebrated Passover that evening (Matthew 26:17–19; Mark 14:12–16; Luke 22:7–15), but John says that the priests, and presumably everyone else, ate the Passover meal on the next evening (John 18:28). This suggests that Jesus ate Passover a day early.

Several other potential scandals marred this final Passover. First, Jesus refused to drink the last cup of wine, only drinking three of the four cups that were essential to the ceremony. Second, he persuaded his disciples to eat some extra bread after the meal had finished, which detracted from the importance of the lamb. And third, Jesus identified himself with the bread and wine in a way that was close to idolatry.

These changes have much more importance than the fact that they are deviations from the normal Passover customs. When Jesus did these things differently, he knew it would stand out in the disciples' memories and that they'd want to know what it meant. Imagine that Jesus was celebrating Christmas but neglected to give any gifts and refused to accept any. We would conclude that he was opposed to Christmas presents, and we might think that he was making a statement against materialism. In the same way, everything that Jesus did contrary to a normal Passover became a message. But in order to find out what this message was, we need to know what would normally happen at a Passover meal.

Although it's surprising to us that Jesus celebrated Passover a day early, it wouldn't actually have been too much of a shock for Jews of the period. We know that some Jews did celebrate Passover a day early in Jesus' time, though even a few decades later no one could remember the reason why.

Two rabbis, Joshua and Ben Bathyra, discussed this question in about AD 90. Ben Bathyra thought it was due to variations in the beginning of a new month. Jews started their months whenever they saw the first sliver of new moon, but sometimes it might be seen in Galilee one night, while fog in Jerusalem prevented it from being seen until the following night. In that case the Galileans would be one day ahead. Rabbi Joshua, however, thought the discrepancy was due to a stretched interpretation of the phrase "between the evenings" (a literal translation of Exodus 12:6). This was normally understood to mean "between the start and end of evening", but some people interpreted it to mean "between one evening and the next". In this case they could therefore eat the Passover meal at any time from the start of the previous evening.

The two rabbis couldn't decide who was right, and modern debates have similarly failed to come to a conclusion. But the fact that the discussion took place shows us that some Jews *did* eat the Passover a day early, just as Jesus did.[1]

If having the Passover meal a day early wasn't actually a real deviation from normal practice, what about the other differences? The Passover rules said that every celebrant should take part in four cups of wine, and that a poor person should even mortgage his warm cloak in order to afford these four cups.[2] And there was also an ancient rule that no food (such as bread) should be eaten after the main meal.[3] However, both these rules were introduced *after* Jesus' day and, in his time, only three cups were compulsory – the fourth was optional. Therefore neither Jesus' introduction of some extra bread at the end of the meal, nor his refusal to drink the fourth cup, was particularly significant either.

The compulsory fourth cup was introduced later to curtail those Jews who wanted to end the Passover meal with a drinking party like the Romans did at their banquets. To accompany this fourth cup, the serving of more bread was added to the ritual. In modern Passover meals this bread is hidden so that the children can go around the room and search for it. The Roman drinking party was known as an *epikômos* and this word gradually changed to *aphikomen* – the modern name for this last part of the Passover meal.

Even when Jesus said "this bread is my body", he wouldn't have caused much comment or consternation among the disciples. It sounds rather mystical to our ears, but the imagery fitted in with the rest of the ritual that went with the meal. The leader said something like: "These bitter herbs are the bitterness our ancestors suffered in Egypt; this brown *charoset* paste is the mortar they used for bricks; and this bowl of salt water is the tears which they wept." When Jesus followed this up with "this bread is my body", the disciples would have wondered what he meant, but it wouldn't have sounded utterly incongruous.

However, there were two aspects of Jesus' last Passover which were totally unprecedented and, for any first-century

Jew, disgusting and scandalous. The first incident was Jesus' insistence on washing his disciples' feet, and this was followed by his designation of the third cup as "my blood". These two events happened right at the start and finish of the meal, and must have utterly scandalized those in the room.

First, a servant came to Jesus with a bowl of water and a towel so that he could ceremonially wash his hands before saying grace. Instead, Jesus tied the towel round his waist, picked up the bowl, and made his way round the table, acting as a servant to all the others. We can measure the shock value of this action by Peter's reaction. He utterly refused to let Jesus wash his feet until Jesus insisted in very strong terms (John 13:8).

After this embarrassment, the meal started as normal with the first cup of wine accompanied by bitter herbs wrapped in bread and dipped in the *charoset* paste. Jesus gave this to Judas, as if to an honoured guest. The second cup of wine was followed by the main meal of lamb, and then the third cup should have ended the meal.

Jesus' introduction of bread before the third cup, saying, "This is my body", was certainly unusual and memorable. But the disciples wouldn't have been truly surprised or scandalized until he took the third cup and blessed it, saying: "This is my blood." Mark implies that they all drank it *before* Jesus spoke these startling words (Mark 14:23–24). This sounds realistic, because it is almost unbelievable that any pious Jew would drink the wine after it had been called "blood".

Drinking blood was the strongest taboo in the Old Testament. It was regarded as almost akin to murder because "the life of a creature is in its blood" (Leviticus 17.3–6, 10–14). Anyone who killed an animal for food without ritually draining all of its blood had to be expelled from Israel. Priests even avoided drinking the red wine that accompanied offerings, even though they could consume the cereals and oil that were given with the same offerings. Perhaps they were worried that someone might think they were drinking the blood so, to prevent this, they ceremonially poured away the wine in view of everyone. This practice is only implied in the Old Testament, but it is stated clearly in later Jewish writing: "He poured out the libation of the blood of the grape at the foot of the altar."[4] It is certain that no Jew would drink wine that was even symbolically "blood".

The message Jesus was giving at the meal is very important because it is what he intended us to remember at Communion or Mass. In behaving like a servant and calling the wine his blood, Jesus was clearly saying that he was both a servant and a sacrifice.

These two roles are related to each other. When Jesus was explaining how he was going to save humanity, he said: "The Son of Man did not come to be served, but to serve, and to give his life as a ransom for many" (Mark 10:45; Matthew 20:28). At his last Passover, a servant brought water to Jesus, but instead of accepting the service of another, Jesus went and served everyone else. And his declaration that the wine was "my blood… which is poured out for many" (Matthew 26:28) is similar to the phrase, "give his life as a ransom for many". The correspondence is close and is unlikely to be a coincidence.

It would have been so easy at this last Passover for Jesus to provoke his disciples to love him, pity him, regard him as a hero, or even as their God. But he aimed for none of these. Instead, Jesus wanted them to remember him doing the job of a servant and giving his whole life for them. The taking of Communion, which we see as a ceremony to remind us of Jesus' greatness and our salvation, had a rather different purpose in his own mind. Jesus was reminding us primarily that he lived as a servant and that he calls his followers to be servants of each other.

For Jesus' followers today, the scandal of the last Passover meal isn't about the changes that he made to it – though they were certainly scandalous at the time. The scandal now is the way in which many parts of the church have subverted Jesus' emphatic message about servanthood by changing this meal into a ceremony which elevates church leaders above the congregation.

Notes

1. The priests knew this would happen and allowed the people to bring their Passover lambs a day early; they pretended it was a peace offering and it was processed in exactly the same way as a Passover offering. See Tosephta Pesachim 4.8; Mishnah Zebachim 1.3.
2. Mishnah Pesachim 10.1.
3. Mishnah Pesachim 10.8.
4. Ben Sira 50.15; Numbers 15:10.

Contemplating Suicide

One of the horrors of Hitler's Germany was Aktion T4 – a programme to carry out "mercy deaths". Its purpose was the elimination of "life unworthy of life", a definition including the mentally or incurably ill and physically disabled adults and children. Death by gassing, injection or starvation was carried out by physicians without consulting the patient. Doctors in Holland were the only ones in the occupied countries who refused to comply with the decree.

Ironically, Holland is now famous for its Euthanasia Act (2002) which legalized a convention practised by the Dutch medical community for over twenty years. Assisted killing is now allowed even for severely disabled children and for depressed patients who are otherwise healthy. Analysis of the figures is disturbing.[1] In 2005 almost 10 per cent of all deaths in Holland were medically assisted. Some studies suggest that another 10 per cent were not officially reported and that physicians acted without consulting patients or relatives in 45 per cent of these cases. As a result, many Dutch citizens carry a card in their wallet in case they are hospitalized, stating their wish that "no treatment be administered with the intention to terminate life".

Euthanasia is threatening to become an acceptable way to commit suicide, and even suicide in the absence of illness is rarely regarded as immoral. In New Testament times suicide was totally respectable among Romans. They regarded it as honourable to end your life if you had brought shame on your family or your legion. Famous Greek and Roman suicides include Pythagoras, Socrates, Zeno, Demosthenes, Marc Antony, and Seneca. Two Roman emperors committed suicide in a single year – Nero and Otho, in AD 68. Their deaths couldn't have been more different. Nero, who was infamous for his tyranny, decided to kill himself when he heard he'd been sentenced to be flogged to death. But he couldn't go through with it, so he asked a companion to show him how to do it by killing himself. When he heard the arrest party approaching he quickly managed to stab his throat, with some help from his secretary. People rioted with joy at the news of his death. However, when Otho killed himself crowds mourned and some of his officers threw themselves on his funeral pyre. He had ended his own life in order to save others by preventing the need for a battle between two rival Roman armies.

Ancient Jews, unlike the Romans, regarded suicide as murder in most instances – God had given life and only he had the right to take it away. In fact, life was so precious that all except three of God's commandments could be broken in order to save your own or someone else's life. The exceptions were idolatry, sexual immorality and murder: committing these was considered worse than death. Perhaps this helps explain why the zealots defending the fortress of Masada committed suicide in AD 73 just before the Romans finally broke in. The men killed their wives and children, and then each other, to avoid rape and torture followed by death or slavery. Their story was told by two women and five children who had managed to hide.

The Old Testament records six suicides,[2] but moral comments are rare in the historical sections of the Bible, so we aren't told whether these suicides were considered right or wrong. The ancient rabbis were clear on the subject, however – suicide was sinful so it couldn't be followed by a proper Jewish burial.[3] This strict ruling was ignored in the case of children and in situations of great "stress", and they considered that King Saul's suicide was excusable for this reason (1 Samuel 31:1–4). However, not many people fall into the same category of stress as Saul, who was mortally wounded, and about to be captured and possibly tortured! In practice, the only funeral rite Jews actually omitted for suicides was the eulogy. The early-second-century rabbi Akiva said the lack of a eulogy meant that Jews neither praised nor defamed a suicide; many interpreted this to mean that they should just quietly forgive them without condoning what they had done.

The New Testament gives a clear message against suicide by saying that we have been bought by Christ who now owns us (1 Peter 1:18), so we don't have the right to throw our life away. This is illustrated by the stories of two very different characters: Judas and Peter. Judas is described as killing himself out of shame for betraying Jesus. There are two conflicting reports about this, one saying that he hanged himself and the other that he died from a fall (Matthew 27:5; Acts 1:18). These aren't impossible to reconcile – perhaps the rope broke and he fell to his death. They show, like the apparently conflicting reports of the resurrection, that the Gospels record witnesses who didn't collude. Judas' action contrasts with Peter who was equally ashamed and guilty about denying Jesus, but rather than "escaping" by killing himself, he repented and sought forgiveness.

That same night, in Gethsemane, Jesus experienced extreme mental anguish and the longing to escape what lay ahead of him. He faced the cruellest form of legal execution as well as the spiritual burden of humanity's sin. He was "grieved and distressed" and said: "My soul is overwhelmed with sorrow to the point of death" (Matthew 26:38). A normal human reaction would be to consider a less painful way out, such as suicide. Of course, for Jesus, the transition of death might have been as easy as his later ascension, which made this temptation even more difficult.

Was Jesus tempted to end his life prematurely? He certainly prayed for a way out of having to die on the cross to deal with human sin (v. 39) and he faced the same kinds of temptations that normal humans do – which enables him to understand us and carry our sins (Hebrews 2:18; 4:15). But we have problems imagining Jesus being suicidal, just as we have difficulty thinking of him having sexual temptations – as portrayed too graphically by film director Martin Scorsese in *The Last Temptation of Christ*. For this reason, most commentators conclude that Jesus suffered extreme distress and sadness without any thoughts of ending his life.

Ancient commentators are even more reticent to acknowledge Jesus' humanity, and say he was grief-stricken simply because his disciples would suffer. However, some modern commentators point out that the Gospel writers deliberately use the same language as Jonah, who also experienced "sorrow to the point of death" when he wished he were dead (Jonah 4:8–9). Jesus didn't just wander through this world *pretending* to be human; he felt the full breadth of emotions – welcome and unwelcome – that we ourselves do.

Feelings of desperation, despair, and the accompanying temptation to commit suicide, are not sinful. No temptation is sinful in itself – only acting on it. But when we suffer from profound sadness or depression we experience self-loathing, and the suicidal temptations increase our feelings of sinfulness. At such times, the thought that Jesus endured some of the same terrible feelings is precious to us.

Even Jesus looked for help from his friends. He didn't simply go off and pray by himself – he took his disciples along and asked the closest three to stay awake with him. Depression often makes us feel isolated – even our close friends and God feel distant from us. At such times, we would do well to try to remember that this is a symptom of depression, rather than the reality of our situation. And, like the friends of desperate people often do, Jesus' disciples misunderstood him and let him down when he needed them most.

The Bible doesn't condone suicide, but it does hold out hope for the suicidal. The Bible uses a carrot, not a stick, for those who feel unable to cope, and are ready to give up. Paul says, "God is faithful; he will not let you be tempted beyond what you can bear. But when you are tempted, he will also provide a way out so that you can stand up under it" (1 Corinthians 10:13). When it feels like the future is unbearable, we can remember that Jesus too felt the same way. This doesn't make the feelings less awful, but we can know that he understands intimately how we are suffering, and he never leaves us to cope alone.

Notes

1. See http://content.nejm.org/cgi/content/full/356/19/1957
2. Abimelech son of Gideon (Judges 9:54), Samson (Judges 16:25–31), Saul (1 Samuel 31:3–4; 1 Chronicles 10:3–4), Saul's squire (1 Samuel 31:5; 1 Chronicles 10:5), Ahithophel (2 Samuel 17:23), Zimri (1 Kings 16:18–19).
3. See the supplement to the Talmud called *Semachot*, which is a euphemistic title meaning "Joy".

Censored Arrest Warrant

The Talmud is a key text in mainstream Judaism in the form of a record of rabbinic discussions about Jewish law, ethics, philosophy, customs and history. Many of the oldest and most valuable of these traditions are in the Babylonian Talmud which compiles documents written in late antiquity (the first to fifth centuries AD). However, all the original references to Jesus in the Babylonian Talmud were censored out in the fifteenth and sixteenth centuries. Surprisingly, perhaps, this was the fault of the church – it certainly wasn't a conspiracy by Jews.

Almost all manuscripts of the Talmud were destroyed in countless book burnings and persecutions. It survived largely thanks to Daniel Bomberg, a sixteenth-century Christian who spent his family fortune and worked tirelessly to print most of the great Jewish works. Because multiple copies were printed these books were not completely eradicated. They were, however, censored. Every book that was printed had to be authorized by the Pope, and the church required publishers to remove everything referring to Jesus before it would give them a licence.

The ancient Jewish writings about Jesus that were removed from the printed copies have survived in only a handful of manuscripts which escaped burning. Most of them were recorded a few centuries after Jesus and are anti-Christian slurs such as descriptions of Mary as a loose woman and Jesus as a disgruntled Jew who learned Gentile magic. It isn't surprising the Pope didn't like them! There is, however, one passage which probably comes from the time of Jesus himself – and, incredibly, it is hugely significant. It is a passage that preserves the original arrest warrant or charge sheet against Jesus.

This passage containing the arrest warrant is likely to be genuine because of the scandal surrounding it. The damage it did to the reputation of the Jews meant that they wouldn't have made it up, and they found it impossible to "bury" because it was too well known. So instead of trying to make people forget about it, the Jewish leaders' solution was to preserve the record, but to exercise some "damage limitation" by adding invented material to deal with most of the things causing them embarrassment.

Unfortunately the censors of the sixteenth century cut out the *whole* passage – the original charge sheet as well as the later rabbis' additions – and it is only recently that scholars have been able to identify the original words. Here is what the censors removed, with the original in bold and the later additions in normal type:

> **On the Eve of Passover they hung Jesu the Nazarine.** And the herald went out before him for 40 days [saying]: "Jesu the Nazarine will go out to be stoned **for sorcery** and misleading **and enticing Israel**. Any who know [anything] in his defence must come and declare concerning him." But no-one came to his defence so they hung him on the Eve of Passover.[1]

This tells us what we already know from the Gospels: Jesus was crucified on the day which ends with the Passover meal in the evening – that is, the 14th of Nisan (see the chapter "Supplanted Passover"). It also tells us something new: he was charged with the two capital offences of "sorcery" and "enticing Israel" – that is, enticing them to idolatry (see Deuteronomy 13:6; 18:10; Exodus 22:18). The words in bold (the original charge sheet) are preserved independently in other Christian and Jewish texts.[2]

The rabbis made later additions to this ancient report to

try to deal with three huge problems implied by it that were extremely damaging to them. The first problem was that according to Jewish law, a trial should not have occurred on a religious holiday. To explain this, the rabbis attempted to make out that they had tried to help Jesus defend himself by giving him extra time to find witnesses to speak on his behalf. They did this by adding in that forty days were given for Jesus to produce witnesses, but no one came forward. (The idea for this may well have come about because a law had been passed after the time of Jesus allowing thirty days for defence witnesses to be found.) By inserting this "extra" detail they tried to imply that they had not only allowed thirty days, but had generously granted a further ten days, after which the trial could not be delayed any longer because Passover was starting. This "editing" of the original made the illegal trial date look like Jesus' fault!

The second problem was that Jesus was killed on a cross, whereas the law of Moses said he should be stoned. It also rubbed in the fact that the Jews weren't in charge – the Romans were, and it was they who decided to crucify him. The rabbis dealt with this embarrassment by inserting the herald's message that Jesus was to be stoned. This made it look as if he was stoned and then hung (i.e. his corpse was hung in public view). Of course, it couldn't have actually happened that way: even if the Jews had stoned Jesus while the Romans weren't looking, they couldn't then advertise their crime by hanging up his body.

The third problem was the one that damaged them the most: the original document charged Jesus with sorcery and this implied that his miracles were genuine – because only genuine sorcery was punished by death. The Jewish leaders would not have reached this conclusion because they were easily taken in by illusions or trickery purporting to be magic. They were, in fact, quite sceptical. For example, one rabbi reported: "I myself saw an Arabian traveller take a sword and cut up a camel; then he rang a bell and the camel arose." Another rabbi saw through it: "Was any blood or dung left behind? If not, it was merely an illusion."[3] The Gospels suggest that the Jewish leaders watched Jesus carefully, and concluded that his miracles were genuine, but were done by Satan's power (Matthew 12:24–26) – that is, they were genuine sorcery.

Later Jewish leaders regretted that this charge was made because it confirmed and strengthened the belief of second-century Jews that Jesus had learned magic in Egypt.[4] Like most people of the time, Jews were intensely interested in magic and they used amulets for warding off evil and illness. They started using Jesus' name for magic and archaeologists have found his name inscribed alongside names of Jewish angels in the second and third centuries.[5]

The rabbis needed to discredit this idea that Jesus had real power so they added a third charge, just after "sorcery": the charge of "misleading" Israel. This was a stroke of genius because the word "misleading" is related to the charge of "enticing Israel" (in Deuteronomy 13:5, 10 it is "lead astray"), but it also adds the suggestion that his sorcery was fake. Of course, that is illogical – because fake sorcery wasn't punishable by death – but it helped to cast doubt on Jesus' miracles.

Both accusations against Jesus – performing miracles using dark powers and leading people astray – are referred to in the Gospels (Mark 3:22; Matthew 12:.24; Luke 11:15; John 7:12). Jesus takes these charges very seriously, answering the first at length (unlike other slurs which he simply ignores), and treating the second as a death threat (John 7:19). We can now see that he was right to do so because both appear on the arrest warrant. But when the rabbis put Jesus on trial and their case went wrong, the High Priest, in exasperation, charged him with blasphemy (Matthew 26:65; Mark 14:64). And when it came to convincing the Romans of his guilt, they resorted to the charge of sedition – saying that he called himself king (Luke 23:2). The Jewish leaders kept quiet about the other two charges, especially "sorcery", because this implied that even they recognized that Jesus' miracles were genuine.

In the end the Gospels declare Jesus guilty as charged: he *did* claim to be king; he *did* claim to be divine; he *did* perform genuine miracles; and he *did* try to lead Israel into a new form of worship (though not idolatry). But if Jesus was who he said he was – the Son of God revealing God in new glory – then his guilt was proof of his mission.

For scholars, the scandal of Jesus' arrest warrant is that this important ancient text was almost lost forever. If it really does include a record of what happened at Jesus' trial, it helps confirm some details in the Gospel record. For Jews, the scandal lies in the rather clumsy cover-up of three inconvenient and embarrassing truths. And for Christians, the scandal lies in the false charges made against Jesus.

The episode is also a scandal for the church because, in forcing Jews to censor their religious texts, it almost lost this valuable piece of history about Jesus which it could have trumpeted as another confirmation of Jesus' divine role. But far worse than that, it continued and encouraged the anti-Semitic sentiments which have led to so many atrocities. In our reactions to Islam and to many modern faiths, it's worth remembering that restrictions of any religion can lead to evil consequences on both sides.

Notes

1. Babylonian Talmud Sanhedrin 43a, Munich Manuscript.
2. Justin Martyr, *Dialogue with Trypho* 69, about AD 150; Babylonian Talmud Sanhedrin 107b, 67a in uncensored manuscripts.

3. Rab talking with Rabbi Hiyya in Babylonian Talmud Sanhedrin 67b.
4. Origen, *Contra Celsum*, i. 28.
5. Gideon Bohak, *Ancient Jewish magic: a history*, Cambridge University Press, 2008, p. 278; John Michael Greer, *The New Encyclopedia of the Occult*, Llewellyn Publications, 2003, p. 248.

Shameful Execution

Over fifty years ago a member of my family was an inmate in a UK prison where executions were occasionally carried out. He told me that on the morning of a hanging, the prisoners would be uncharacteristically quiet. Even though they didn't witness what was happening, it affected them all. Perhaps they were thinking more deeply about their own lives, or maybe they were simply thankful that they'd escaped this fate themselves.

UK society has largely moved away from wanting capital punishment, but executions were very popular up until the mid 1800s when they were carried out in public. So many people used to skip work to attend the eight major execution days in London that they were made into official holidays.

Jewish society in Jesus' day had a contradictory attitude towards the death penalty. The leaders tried to avoid prescribing the death sentence, even when it was the punishment set down in the Old Testament. Most of their capital offences – from being "a glutton and drunkard" to breaking the Sabbath (Deuteronomy 21:20; Exodus 31:14) – were punished by no more than a sin offering in Jesus' day. By the end of the first century some leaders of Judaism said that they *never* wanted to apply the death penalty.[1] In modern Israel there is still the option of the death penalty, but in practice it remains virtually abolished – it has only been applied once, for the Nazi war criminal Adolf Eichmann.

Jewish crowds didn't think in the same way as their leaders, and they could be enticed to stone someone. This was how Stephen died (Acts 8:58), how the adulteress would have died if

Jesus hadn't rescued her (John 8:3–9), and it almost happened to Jesus on more than one occasion (Luke 4:29; John 8:59; 10:31). When it came to Jesus' crucifixion, it wasn't difficult to make the crowds cry out for blood.

Crucifixion was such a despised form of death that Roman citizens were almost always excused this punishment; instead they were forced into exile or allowed to commit suicide. Even non-citizens were normally executed by more "pleasant" means such as garrotting, slitting the throat, or being killed by gladiators or animals in the Games; only the worst criminals were crucified. Crucifixion was the most painful, prolonged and disgraceful form of execution which has ever been carried out as a legal sanction. Even Roman law eventually banned it as being too barbaric.

In Jewish eyes, the scandal of crucifixion was due more to its shameful and humiliating consequences than to the prolonged pain and suffering it inflicted. The facts of this are very unpleasant, so please skip the rest of this paragraph if you think you might be offended. In unprofessional hangings where the neck is not broken, a person dies of gradual asphyxiation, and this can result in an erection and defecation. Hitler's SS used to deliberately hang victims slowly to enhance this public disgrace. Crucifixion, which was death by very slow asphyxiation, was made even more shameful because the victims were stripped naked.

Although Old Testament law prescribed stoning for blasphemy, Jewish leaders couldn't carry this sentence out on Jesus because the occupying Roman army was responsible for executions (see John 18:31). On this occasion, however, they were probably happy that the Romans were in charge because they expected that a death by crucifixion would ruin Jesus' reputation for ever. They probably believed that the scandal of a crucifixion would make it impossible for Jesus' followers to venerate him after his death. As far as they were concerned, it was the perfect end for a false Messiah.

Jesus was by no means the only Jew to be crucified. The Romans regularly executed a few of the worst criminals in this way as a powerful deterrent to others. They were mostly "insurrectionists" (i.e. terrorists), so the two criminals crucified with Jesus shouldn't be described in translation as mere "thieves". There were two mass crucifixions in Jerusalem: 800 Pharisees were crucified as traitors in 267 BC, and when Jerusalem was besieged in AD 70, the Romans terrorized the inhabitants by crucifying anyone they caught escaping – as many as 500 per day!

Although Jesus' death on the cross was not unique, few (if any) underwent both flogging and crucifixion. This flogging, so graphically illustrated in the film *The Passion of the Christ*, was designed to do as much damage as possible without killing the victim. Pieces of metal tied into the whip thongs tore gouges out of the back. According to John, Pilate ordered the flogging in the hope that it would appease the crowd enough to prevent them wanting a crucifixion (John 19:1–6). That didn't work, so Jesus ended up with a double punishment.

In the Old Testament, an added way to show that a crime was utterly heinous was to execute someone and then hang their body on a tree instead of burying it. This signified that they were cursed by God – perhaps it implied that God didn't want them even in the world of the dead. So for Jews, an added scandal of Jesus' crucifixion was that "hanging on a tree" was a specific indication of God's curse. The leaders could use this to show that Jesus was not sent by God. However, Christian preachers like Paul turned its meaning around by pointing out that God did indeed curse Jesus on the cross and that Jesus accepted God's curse on behalf of humanity (Galatians 3:13).

The scandal of crucifixion did almost succeed in blackening

Jesus' reputation. Although the New Testament made positive theological points about the scandal of the cross (Galatians 5:11; Hebrews 12:2), early Christians were publicly quiet about it. Early church writers emphasized the teaching and example of Jesus rather than his death on the cross. The symbol of the cross is totally absent from Christian art at that time; we find pictures of Jesus as the Good Shepherd, as a teacher, and as a sacrificed lamb, but never as a crucified man.

The only picture of the crucifixion which survives from the first three centuries was crudely scratched on a plaster wall in Rome. It depicts a crucified man with the head of an ass, and another man looking on. The caption reads: "Alexamanos worships his god." This demonstrates the almost impossible task of persuading people to honour someone who was crucified. For most people, the crucifixion was the clinching argument against following Jesus. As a result, the symbol of the cross didn't come into widespread use till Constantine saw it in the sky just before a battle, with the revelation: "In this sign, conquer."

Today the cross has become respectable – all the blood, faeces and shreds of skin are cleaned off. We have gold crosses encrusted with jewels, crosses made of neon lights, and huge concrete crosses. People draw a cross on buildings, on letterheads and on babies' heads. Others wear it as religious jewellery or merely as decoration. The church appropriated the most distinctive logo ever invented, but we seem to have forgotten what it means.

Jesus suffered the most disgusting, painful and shameful form of legal execution ever practised, but passing centuries have blunted the impact of the cross. In his death, Jesus identified himself with the worst of criminals and told his followers to visit prisoners as though they were visiting him (Matthew 25:31–40). Although some Christian organizations continue this practice, it has somehow moved outside the remit of most churches, who fail to see any link between Jesus and criminals. Has the church, along with the cross, become just too respectable?

Notes
1. Mishnah Makkot 1.10.

Embarrassing Resurrection

I love the old Jewish joke about a rabbi who sneaked off to a golf club one Sabbath. God said to the angels: "Watch how I punish him." As they watched, the rabbi performed a perfect swing from his tee and was rewarded with a hole-in-one. The angels said: "How is that a punishment?" And God replied: "Who can he tell?"

The disciples must have felt like that on the first Sunday when they saw Jesus alive. This was wonderful – but who was it safe to tell? And who would believe it? If they tried to convince people, they'd get into dangerous trouble. The good news that we rejoice in, was a scandal to any first-century Greek or Roman. In their place, we might have concluded it was better to keep this knowledge to ourselves, but fortunately the disciples thought differently.

Romans and Greeks simply didn't believe in any kind of resurrection. We might think that with the myths about gods and demigods they inherited from the old Greek religions, they'd have been prepared to accept stories of life after death, but by the first century they had a philosophical attitude to the concept. Although some believed in the stories that happened in the distant past, no one except religious fanatics and madmen was willing to accept the possibility of such things in the present. So when Paul tried telling the philosophers in Athens about "Jesus and the resurrection", the concept of resurrection was so off their radar that they assumed he was talking about two gods: "Jesus and *Anastasia*" (Greek for "resurrection"). When Paul said he did mean Jesus' literal resurrection, most of them simply laughed (Acts 17:18, 32).

The Jews had different problems when it came to Jesus' resurrection. They believed that God *could* raise someone from the dead (it had happened a few times in the Old Testament), but they didn't expect the Messiah to be raised. The prophecies about this are only obvious in retrospect – which is why his disciples were so astounded when Jesus pointed out these particular scriptures (Luke 24:25–27). Also, they thought that being crucified was a mark of God's curse, so Jesus would be the last person for God to favour in this way. This, together with their expectations about the Messiah being victorious over his enemies, made the Jews especially reluctant to accept his resurrection.

Even Christians had problems believing it. The largest section in Paul's long letters to the Corinthians is where he tries to convince them about the resurrection (1 Corinthians 15). Reading between the lines, he is replying to those who said the resurrection was just too hard to accept, and evangelism would be much easier without it. Paul answers, however, that it is the heart of the Gospel! He realized that they rejected it because they didn't understand it. Like the believers at Thessalonica, some thought that you could only be resurrected to heaven if you were still alive or, at least, had an intact corpse (1 Thessalonians 4:13–16). Paul had to explain that though the corpse may be raised in a corrupted state, it is replaced by a new body which is considerably better (1 Corinthians 15:38–53).

Jews in Jesus' day knew about decayed corpses. When their relatives had been dead for about a year, they pulled the rags off the shrivelled body, scraped the bones clean, then collected them in an ossuary – a small stone box for this purpose – and put them in the family vault. Most adult males would have done this gruesome task at least once so they knew that the resurrection wasn't just re-animation of a corpse. Even if all the bones were present, God would need to rebuild the body completely (as in Ezekiel 37). Paul said the new body was as different from the old body as a seed and the plant which grows from it (1 Corinthians 15:35–37).

Archaeologists keep finding new collections of ossuaries and, of course, the search has long been on to find a family tomb inscribed with the three names "Joseph", "Mary" and "Jesus". They haven't yet done so, but I expect they will, because these were such very common names. At the time of Jesus, one in four women were called Mary, one in ten men were called Joseph, and one in twenty-five were called Jesus. So, for every average tomb of ten ossuaries, there is a 4.7 per cent chance that it will contain a Mary, Joseph and Jesus together. Even though it will be based on totally flawed evidence, a find like this will sadly cause many people to dismiss the resurrection. There are also, however, serious problems in the historical account of Jesus' resurrection that made it easy for people to dismiss the story at the time, and subsequently.

The first problem is that the primary witnesses were women, and their testimony was worth only half that of a man in a Jewish court – and worth nothing at all in the minds of many ancient Jews. Second, the Gospel reports don't easily cohere. For example, John says Mary Magdalene came to the tomb, Matthew says that she was accompanied by Mary the mother of Joanna, Mark adds that Salome joined them, and Luke says the third person was called Joanna. A third problem is that people didn't always recognize Jesus. In other words, they would fail the first question put to a witness in court: "Do you recognize this person?" A lawyer in court would highlight these as scandals that undermined the case.

However, to a historian, it is these scandals which make

the resurrection believable. Anyone merely inventing the story would have told it differently. They'd say that the main witnesses were men who recognized Jesus immediately, and they'd make sure that the witnesses' stories tallied with each other. Of course, the four different accounts about who came to the tomb can be easily explained – they didn't each mention everyone who was there, and Joanna was also called Salome – but an invented story wouldn't have left any possibility for such confusion in the first place.

The official explanation given by the Jewish religious leaders for Jesus' missing body was that it was stolen by Jesus' followers while the soldiers slept, but Matthew has a counter-claim that the soldiers and their superiors were bribed to say this by Jewish leaders. This claim and counter-claim are likely to be genuine because Matthew wouldn't invent a plausible explanation that would merely put doubt in the mind of the reader, though he would respond to it if this explanation already existed.

So which side is telling the truth? Here again, potential scandal helps historians to decide: the punishment for falling asleep on duty was death,[1] so no soldier would admit to it unless they knew they weren't at risk from such punishment by their superior officers. This story certainly didn't originate with soldiers who wanted to be honest about their failings – the explanation of bribery is much more believable.

A Roman inscription in the Bibliothèque Nationale de France suggests that even Caesar heard the soldiers' story. This two-foot-square marble, dated to the mid first century, is called the "Nazareth Inscription" because it was found there in 1878, though it may have originated elsewhere in Palestine. It says, in the name of Caesar, that:

> Graves and tombs... must remain undisturbed... If any person has destroyed or in any manner extracted those who were buried to another place... or has moved sepulchre-sealing stones... they should suffer capital punishment as a tomb-breaker.

It is in Koine Greek, so it was directed at the common people.

Jesus' resurrection may have prompted this inscription because it doesn't threaten death for robbing graves, but for moving bodies. And it is only concerned with Jewish tombs, because Roman tombs contained urns of ashes, not bodies. Why would the emperor be so concerned about Jewish corpses being moved from one tomb to another? No similar edict is found elsewhere, and Roman law was generally unconcerned about disturbing non-Roman tombs. It is hard to find any explanation for this inscription except the emperor trying to prevent more crazy Jewish religions like Christianity springing up.

Paradoxically, modern science makes it easier for people today to believe that God can raise Jesus, and that he can even raise us after our bodies have decayed. The concept of the genetic code helps us understand how God might rebuild our bodies, without the scars of living; and making hard-drive back-ups helps us to understand how God might preserve the contents of our mind and memory. And yet we find it as hard to convince people about the resurrection as even the earliest Christians did. Evangelism might still be so much easier without the resurrection but, as Paul said... what would be the point?

Notes

1. For Roman soldiers see Polybius *Histories* 6.36–37; for Jewish Temple guards see Mishnah Sanhedrin 9.6. The latter does not mention the specific charge of falling asleep but includes charges which are militarily less serious.

PART 2

SCANDALS AMONG JESUS' FRIENDS

Mary Magdalene

Rather than locking up the mentally ill in "lunatic asylums", nowadays we try to support them in the community. Society has changed, and few people fear those with mental illnesses as they did in past generations – though we still have severe prejudices. Those who have suffered from this type of illness are often advised not to disclose it in their CV, and most people would admit to being uneasy visiting a psychiatric ward, even though about 10 per cent of the population need medical help for mental illness during their lifetime. However, the discrimination experienced by sufferers today is nothing compared to the utter misunderstanding and ostracism of the mentally ill in ancient times.

Mary Magdalene came to Jesus in a mess. Luke says that she had seven demons which Jesus cast out (Luke 8:2). Some believe that these "demons" were an ancient description of mental illness, while others think they were evil spiritual entities, but either interpretation means that she was displaying some very severe symptoms of mental illness. She would have been a feared outcast who was despised by the rest of the community.

Mary Magdalene is an important individual in the four Gospels, and her significance grew with time. She is the only person in the Bible to have witnessed Jesus' crucifixion, burial and resurrection (Matthew 27:65, 61; 28:1), and the resurrected Jesus sent her with a message for the apostles. As a result, in various early church literature, she became known as "the apostle to the apostles" and was described as one "whose heart is raised to the kingdom of heaven more than all".[1]

In the two centuries following the writing of the New Testament there was a creative outburst of early church literature which attempted to fill in the "gaps" left in the Gospel accounts – rather like fan fiction develops after a cult TV series ends with unanswered questions. Mary Magdalene figured highly in this literature because she was female, of apparent importance in the Gospels, and yet almost nothing was known about her. These writings also explored aspects of Jesus' life that the New Testament Gospels had neglected, such as what happened during his childhood and his teaching on concepts of the soul and the afterlife.

Early church leaders eventually suppressed these writings when they found that believers were getting confused between them and the canonical Gospels. They eventually published an official list of the twenty-seven books of the New Testament at the Synod of Hippo in AD 393. This list was important, not so much for defining the New Testament (about which there was already general agreement), but for identifying the newer writings as different – that is, not part of the scriptural canon. A number of these later documents may have been burned at the behest of some of the church leaders, but most probably perished simply because, unlike the New Testament, few people bothered to make copies.

Some of this literature survived in the extreme dry conditions of North African deserts, but elsewhere the papyri fell apart due to time and neglect. In 1945, at Nag Hammadi in southern Egypt, a sealed ceramic jar was found containing a hoard of ancient papyri that consisted of a lot of this literature. Other material continues to turn up occasionally, such as the *Gospel of Mary* at a Cairo bazaar in 1896 or the recently discovered *Gospel of Judas*. From these we can trace some of the development of the Mary Magdalene story.

In the North African church, Mary was gradually portrayed in terms of her having been a disciple and male. First, in the *Gospel of Thomas* (about AD 100), she is described as being "among" the disciples, and when Peter complains that she is female, Jesus says he will make her male (*Thomas* 115). And in a question-and-answer session between Jesus and his disciples in the *Pistis Sophia* (written around AD 150), more than half the questions are posed by Mary Magdalene. By about AD 200 the *Gospel of Mary* portrays Peter admitting to her that "the Saviour loved you more than the rest of women" and asking if she knew anything Jesus hadn't told him or the other disciples (though when she describes a vision she had, he rejects it). Written around the same time, the *Gospel of Philip* describes Jesus as regularly greeting Mary "with a kiss on the…" This tantalizing gap is caused by ants having eaten a hole in the parchment!

Most translators fill the gap with the word "mouth" because that was the normal way for men to greet each other, as it still is in many Arab cultures – though it would be indecent to kiss a woman (even your wife) in public. The significance of this phrase is that Jesus supposedly treated Mary like a man – something that would have been highly shocking.

Some modern Western authors such as Dan Brown have not only treated these late writings as if they were history, but have also misunderstood the cultural significance of this form of greeting with a kiss, concluding that Jesus treated Mary like a female lover – and in some novels she is portrayed as the wife of Jesus and the mother of his children. Some ancient authors concluded that Mary was actually "the beloved disciple" of John's Gospel[2] – despite the fact that Mary appears *with* this disciple in John 20:1–2.

Meanwhile, in the West, Mary's story was developed in a

different direction when the church gave her a tacky past – that of a prostitute. It did this by amalgamating her story with those of two other women: first, Mary of Bethany, the sister of Martha, who anointed Jesus' feet with perfume; and second, the "sinner" who wept tears over Jesus' feet and dried them with her hair before she then anointed them (John 12:1–8; Luke 7:37–50). The two stories seem to have such strikingly similar "unusual" features that to us it might look as if they record the same event, but these events were not at all unusual – they occurred at every formal meal (though normally the head was anointed rather than the feet). Washing feet was as common as taking someone's coat and anointing someone's feet would show extra attention akin to taking someone's shoes and bringing them slippers. For the ancient reader, the details that stood out in these stories were that Mary expended a whole bottle of expensive oil on Jesus while the "sinner" used her hair as a towel to dry his feet. They were clearly different women, and there is no reason to confuse either of them with Mary Magdalene.

Unfortunately this new back story for Mary stuck. It became official in a sermon by Pope Gregory the Great in 591 and was popularized by Jacobus de Voragine in *The Golden Legend* – a collection of legends about the major saints written around 1260. It continued to be official Catholic teaching until the 1969 edition of the Missal reversed it, although Mary Magdalene is still a Catholic patron saint for fallen women. This version of her story was the basis for erotic Christian art by artists such as Da Vinci and Titian.[3]

The Eastern church never amalgamated the different women called Mary. Perhaps they realized the confusion was due to the popularity of the name – about a quarter of all women in Jesus' society were called "Mary". However, they did add one interesting legend which is still remembered today. The story is that Mary gained an audience with the Roman Emperor Tiberius to proclaim the Gospel. Holding an egg in her hand she said: "Christ is risen." Tiberius retorted, "That's as likely as your egg turning red", but before he had finished speaking the egg did turn red. This legend is still celebrated by the tradition of painting eggs at Easter.

In all these stories about Mary Magdalene, the New Testament detail that she was the woman "from whom seven demons had come out" has been almost completely ignored. Even when it *is* mentioned, it is submerged by the stories of her life as a prostitute.

It's this rewriting of her history that is the real scandal surrounding Mary Magdalene. It implies that the church believes it is better for her to have been a repentant prostitute than to have been a mad woman. In other words, it wants to avoid having mental illness in the history of a favourite saint.

Mental illness is still a stigma in the church, as in the rest of society. Arguably, the church made this worse in the past by supposedly supporting witch trials, though it later took a leading role in combating such superstition. In the last two centuries the church has been at the forefront in helping the mentally ill through church-run institutions, and it has worked to remove the social stigma of mental illness. Nevertheless, we cannot escape the fact that by inventing a different past for Mary Magdalene it may have significantly delayed the improvement of attitudes towards the mentally ill. We'll never know what difference it might have made if it had embraced the true story of Mary's dramatic healing.

Notes

1. *Pistis Sophia* 17, about AD 150. She is first called "apostle to the apostles" in Hippolytus' *On the Song* 25.6, about AD 200, though this is a conflation with Mary the sister of Martha.

2. The second and third century gospels of Mary and Philip both refer to Mary Magdalene as the disciple who was loved above all others, and this may be based on John's reference to the "beloved disciple".

3. Da Vinci and Titian's provocatively topless paintings are at www.thenazareneway.com/marymagdelene_narrowweb__300x401,0.jpg and www.titian-tizianovecellio.org/Mary-Magdalen-Repentant.html.

Judas Iscariot

I've heard criminologists described as people who find "excuses" for criminal behaviour. I'm sure that those who commit crimes can be influenced by things such as family background, poverty, and being crossed in love, but how much can these excuse a crime? What is the difference between a "cause" and an "excuse"? The law is built on the understanding that we all have free choice – whatever the provocation, ultimately we are responsible for our own actions. However, courts also take "mitigating circumstances" into account, so background factors such as a broken and unstable home environment can significantly reduce a sentence.

If Judas Iscariot was put on trial today would he be found guilty of cold-hearted betrayal for cash, or would the judge find there were mitigating circumstances? Have the Gospels scandalously heaped blame on Judas when he doesn't deserve it?

Many scriptwriters, novelists and theologians have struggled with the character of Judas. Some think he wanted to provoke Jesus into action – to create a situation whereby Jesus would have to show his hand and lead Israel against the Romans. Perhaps he acted as a result of disappointment that Jesus hadn't started a rebellion after his triumphal march into Jerusalem. Surely it had been the perfect time to act, with the crowds hailing him as a conquering ruler, shouting out "*Hosanna*" – just as they had greeted previous new rulers (see the chapter "Disruptive Worship"). When his plan failed and Jesus let himself be arrested and killed, it was a total surprise and shock to Judas.

Others think that Judas misunderstood what the priests wanted, that he believed they were just hiring him as a guide to take them to Jesus so they could talk privately with him. It's difficult to accept this view since the amount they paid Judas – 30 shekels – would have been four months' wages for a labourer, or about £5,000 or $7,500 in present-day money. This was much more than you'd pay to a guide.

We cannot be certain what Judas believed would happen as a result of his actions, but John's Gospel is clear about his motive – it was greed. At the home of Lazarus, Mary poured expensive perfume over Jesus' feet – worth about £15,000 or $22,500 today (enough to buy five bottles of the world's most expensive perfume, Clive Christian's "No.1"!). Judas objected to this, saying that the money could have fed the poor. John comments: "He did not say this because he cared about the poor but because he was a thief; as keeper of the money bag, he used to help himself to what was put into it" (John 12:6). Jesus replied to Judas: "This [perfume] was intended for my burial; you'll always have the poor" (John 12:7–8). John doesn't record Judas' reaction, but Mark says straight after this incident: "Then Judas went to the chief priests to betray Jesus" (Mark 14:10). In Matthew we can see even more clearly that money was part of Judas' motive, because he asked the priests: "What are you willing to give me if I hand him over to you?" (Matthew 26:15). Perhaps the incident with the perfume made Judas regard Jesus as too unworldly to ever achieve anything. Or maybe he realized the end was near and he had only one chance to cash in.

But were there "mitigating circumstances"? Did Judas jump or was he pushed? Jesus knew what Judas was planning – he told everyone about the coming betrayal at his Last Supper. When his disciples all denied they'd do such a thing, including Judas, Jesus turned to him privately and said: "Go, do it quickly"

(John 13:27). Judas then went straight off to the priests, leaving the others thinking he was giving Passover money to the poor. All four Gospels say that Jesus knew what would happen because of the Old Testament prophecies (Matthew 26:24; Mark 14:21; Luke 22:22; John 13:18), and three of them add the ominous comment about Judas: "It would have been better for him if he had not been born."

Would Judas' barrister be able to cite mitigating circumstances in his defence? One argument is that he didn't have any choice about what happened – it had all been foretold in prophecies. God seems to have picked him out as someone who had to do the dirty deed, whether he wanted to or not.

In fact the prophecies do not specify the name of the betrayer and they don't even say there would be a betrayal at all, let alone who would be betrayed. In the prophecy about thirty pieces of silver (Matthew 27:9) there is nothing about Judas or betrayal. The clearest prophecy is Psalm 41:9: "Even my close friend, someone I trusted, one who shared my bread, has lifted up his heel against me." The phrase "lifted up his heel" meant anything from "played a mean trick" to "betrayed" (it's similar to the dated American idiom, "he's a heel"). But the context isn't where you'd look for a prediction about Jesus' betrayal: it is a psalm written by someone desperately ill who knows that his enemies hope he will die.

This prophecy only fits the facts after they have happened, and even then it isn't very clear. Some people therefore conclude that it wasn't a real prophecy and the Gospel writers just said it was, because it happened to fit. But another way of seeing it is as a prophecy that allowed for free choice. A prophecy that named Judas or described him too clearly wouldn't give him the freedom to make his own decision, but written in the way it was – a prophecy which could only be identified after the event – it didn't influence Judas. God, who can see the future as clearly as the past, could have planted it in the mind of the psalmist for the same reason that Jesus warned his disciples about his coming death: so that when it happened they would still trust that he was in control (John 14:29).

A further plea for mitigating circumstances might be that Judas was nothing more than a puppet of God and/or Satan. In Exodus we read that when Moses pleaded with Pharaoh to let the Israelites go, "God hardened his heart" so that God's glory would be seen in the nation's dramatic escape. God did this nine times (Exodus 4:21; 7:3; 9:12; 10:1, 20, 27; 11:10; 14:4, 8), but it also says three times that Pharaoh hardened his own heart (Exodus 8:15, 32; 9:34). This has been understood by some to mean that God manipulates people to carry out his will. But "hardening your heart" means "being stubborn" – rather like the modern idiom "stiffening your resolve". So when God "hardened" Pharaoh's heart he wasn't prescribing what Pharaoh would do, he was merely stiffening Pharaoh's resolve to do what he'd already decided – making him stick to his decision. It was a way of saying that despite Pharaoh's decision, Israel shouldn't be worried; God was still in ultimate control.

If Judas had decided against betraying Jesus someone else might have done the deed. But Judas was on the same path to self-destruction as Pharaoh. When Jesus said, "Do it quickly", he wasn't pushing Judas into it – he was merely saying: "I know what you're planning, so let's get it over with." Judas had already made his decision and taken the money; he jumped rather than being pushed. And he ended up jumping off a cliff and hanging himself (Matthew 27:5; Acts 1:18). Before he did so, he tried returning the money (Matthew 27:3), but I don't think this was genuine repentance. Peter repented to Jesus after his denial; in contrast, Judas merely regretted what he'd done. If he repented to anyone, it was to himself.

When we hurt a friend or do something clearly wrong, we look for someone to blame: "They made me angry"; "I was punishing them for what they've done to others"; "Someone else made me do it", and so on. I don't think I've ever said to myself that "God made me do it", but this is just a matter of degrees. It is so easy to blame others and so hard to blame ourselves for our own stupidity or selfishness. I haven't betrayed a friend like Judas did, but I know deep down that I could. I've often agreed with a disparaging comment made about a friend by someone I wanted to impress. What's that, if it isn't betrayal?

Second-rate Disciples

My family and I love the saga about rabbits, *Watership Down*. We even named our two rabbits Bigwig and Fiver. Bigwig was the strong fighter who defeated the terrifying leader of the rival warren, General Woundwort. I remember the thrill of the fight between the two opponents when Woundwort realizes how strong Bigwig is, and says that the warren was right to choose him as leader. But Bigwig responds: "I serve someone greater than me." Woundwort assumes from this that Bigwig's leader must be even bigger and stronger, so he becomes completely dispirited and soon loses the fight. But actually Bigwig's leader wasn't a great fighter – his greatness lay in an ability to lead those who were smarter and stronger than himself. Woundwort's defeat showed that he didn't understand this key aspect of leadership. Corporate strategists concentrate on hiring the brightest and best, and ancient rabbis did the same. Their reputation was enhanced by accepting only the very best disciples.

Jesus was different. He invited ridicule and scandal by picking a motley and disreputable bunch of disciples. They were nobodies, with apparently few talents. We don't know much about most of them, which says a lot in itself, and what we do know doesn't inspire confidence. They included a former Roman collaborator (the "tax man" Matthew or Levi); a former member of a terrorist group (Simon "the Zealot"); Thomas, who famously suffered from doubt (even doubting Jesus!); and the brothers John and James, who were nicknamed "Sons of Thunder" because they had considerable problems with anger management!

And Judas turned out to be a huge embarrassment to the early church, because the one whom Jesus trusted as treasurer ended up betraying him for money.

The other disciples did nothing worth noting in the Gospels or in the rest of the New Testament. Not many of the leaders of the early church were among the twelve, for instance: Stephen, Philip, James the brother of Jesus, Luke, Silas, Barnabas and (most significantly) Paul, all came along later. Apart from a few dubious mentions in later church stories, most of Jesus' actual disciples disappeared into obscurity.

In contrast, famous rabbis in Jesus' day were praised for the quality of their disciples. The disciples of Hillel (a rabbi who lived just before Jesus) included Jonathan ben Uzziel and Johanan ben Zakkai. They were the greatest teachers of their day who were reputed to have rescued and rebuilt Judaism after the destruction of the Temple in AD 70. Hillel's disciples also included Judah ben Sarifai and Mattithiah ben Margalot. The stories about them are of a courageous pair who led riots against Herod when he fixed a Roman eagle on the Temple gates. These details may not be historical, but they illustrate the fact that the greatness of a rabbi was supposed to be reflected in his disciples.

At the time of Jesus, the word "rabbi" (which means "my master/teacher") wasn't an official title; it was like the word "reverend" which used to be a term of respect but has now become a title for someone ordained, and usually trained at theological college. "Rabbi" didn't become a recognized professional title until after Jerusalem was destroyed, so being called "rabbi" didn't mean Jesus needed to have had any formal training. He lived at a time when the roles of rabbis and disciples were still being worked out, and we have to be careful not to put later rules and customs back into our reading of his life. Nevertheless, we have lots of clues about what discipleship was like in those early days.

Although a rabbi could have an occupation, being a disciple was a full-time activity and dedicated disciples were expected to give their whole lives to study. Scholarship was so important that they were even allowed to neglect their wives for up to a month at a time,[1] though Paul warned Christians not to follow this practice (1 Corinthians 7:3–5). Peter set a different example by taking his wife with him on missions (1 Corinthians 9:5).

If a disciple didn't have private means, he had to live very simply. According to a later story, Hillel was so poor when he was a disciple that he couldn't afford the entrance fee to attend his master's lectures. On one occasion he almost froze to death by lying in the snow outside an upstairs lecture room window in order to listen in. In a similar way, Jesus' disciples had to give up their livelihoods and homes to follow Jesus, and they survived on the occasional generosity of others. Jesus, unlike other rabbis, shared the privations of his disciples – he was as homeless and dependent on others as all of them (Matthew 8:20).

As well as a group of close disciples, rabbis also had a larger following who merely attended their public lectures and adopted their rules for living. Hillel supposedly had eighty disciples, so these couldn't have been part of his daily retinue. Similarly, Jesus had seventy disciples, though they didn't just listen to his public lectures – he taught them to preach and pray and sent them out to the many villages in pairs (Luke 10:1).

A rabbi's small inner circle of disciples followed them around constantly in order to emulate them exactly in every circumstance. Sometimes their pupils went to extreme lengths in order to copy them. Simeon ben Azzai recorded three things he learned by following his rabbi into a privy: you should sit rather than stand, you should not face towards the Temple, and you should clean yourself with your left hand. "Too much information!" I can hear you shout, but a disciple considered it his duty to pry. Rabbi Kahana recalled being thrown out of his teacher's house for prying too much. He was dragged out from under a bed where he was making notes about how his rabbi was making love to his wife![2]

Jesus, too, had an inner circle. His first disciples were all uneducated fishermen but, instead of waiting to find better candidates, he made three of them – Peter, James and John – his core group. They shadowed Jesus and learned exactly how to live in the Kingdom of God. They alone witnessed special events like Jesus' transfiguration and bringing the synagogue leader's daughter back to life (Mark 5:37; 9:2). And when Jesus faced his toughest hour, he chose these three to be near him in Gethsemane (Mark 14:33). So, as well as witnessing Jesus' triumphs, they saw him at his weakest moments too.

Jesus gave his top disciple, Simon, the nickname "Peter", saying that he would be a "rock"– a foundation – of the church (Matthew 16:17–19). Jesus was probably being ironic, because "peter" (*petros*) actually means "a pebble", not "a rock". I wonder whether he meant that Peter would *become* a rock, but that to start with he would be as annoying as a small pebble in a sandal. It was Peter who came out with the silly suggestion of putting up a tent on the mount of transfiguration for Moses and Elijah to live in (Matthew 17:4), and he was the one who stupidly agreed to pay the unbiblical annual Temple tax, which Jesus then had to miraculously provide inside a fish (Matthew 17:24–27). You'd think that the story of walking on water would make *anyone* look good, but instead we see Peter having lots of bluster and little faith. If the Gospels were a movie, Peter would more often than not provide the comic relief.

Peter also seemed to be the person who frustrated Jesus more than all the other disciples, perhaps because he'd given him such an important role. When Jesus revealed his plan for salvation, it was Peter who voiced Satan's temptation to avoid suffering (Matthew 16:20–23) and Jesus reprimanded Peter severely. Other disciples could ask Jesus to explain parables, and he was happy to do so, but when Peter asked on one occasion, Jesus rounded on him and said: "Are you still so thick?" (Matthew 15:16). And when the inner three let him down so badly in Gethsemane, Jesus specifically asked Peter why he had fallen asleep (Matthew 26:40). It seems as though Peter could never do anything right.

A rabbi's top disciples were supposed to be those who were the most diligent and brought the greatest praise to their teacher. Hillel's disciple Johanan was known as "a plastered cistern which never spills a drop" – that is, he had a watertight mind which never forgot a word. I inscribed this phrase on a gift for my doctoral supervisor – the modern equivalent of a disciple's gift for his rabbi. It was only later that I anxiously wondered if he knew the saying; if not, he might think "plastered" was an insinuation about drunkenness! Fortunately, his perfect memory recalled it instantly. Johanan was a credit to his rabbi, but Jesus' disciples certainly didn't bring him credit even at the end of their training: when the top scholars examined Peter and John, they concluded they were "uneducated and ignorant" (Acts 4:13). This was the greatest insult you could give to a disciple and his teacher because it implied that they hadn't been taught well and hadn't learned well.

Rabbis taught their disciples by making them memorize their words. A good disciple would keep repeating the words of his master until they were thoroughly embedded in his brain. A lazy disciple was one who stopped after a mere 100 repetitions![3] To help them learn, the rabbi would deliver teaching in memorable groups of short sayings – teaching which was abbreviated as much as possible. The disciples could later expand these succinct versions to make them more intelligible when they explained the teaching. The Sermon on the Mount in Matthew contains this kind of teaching using three series of repetitious sayings: "Blessed are…" (Matthew 5); "You have heard… but I say to you…" (Matthew 6); and "When you… do it this way…" (Matthew 7). The slight differences in Luke's versions are the types of variation which occur when you expand an abbreviated saying – going into it in more depth – as well as differences due to translation from Jesus' Aramaic into Greek.

Rabbis taught in upper rooms, on the steps of the Temple, in olive groves – anywhere, in fact – just like Jesus did. They taught both in public and in private and sometimes their private teaching was different from what they said in public. We see this particularly in the teaching of Rabbi Johanan ben Zakkai. He was in Galilee at the same time as Jesus, so they probably heard each other teach. Johanan faced a lot of questions from non-Jews. His replies were clever, but were actually no more than trick answers; he gave the real answers to his disciples privately.[4]

Jesus also conducted private teaching sessions with his disciples as well as his public teaching (Matthew 13:36; 15:15; Mark 4:34; 7:17) and he, too, employed trick answers (Matthew 21:23–27; 22:17–21). However, unlike other rabbis, Jesus only gave trick answers to trick questions, and his private teaching didn't contradict what he said publicly. As he said at his trial, he had taught everything openly (John 18:20). He hadn't wanted his disciples to possess any secret knowledge or insight that wasn't available to anyone else. They were simply ordinary people who wanted to follow Jesus, and anyone was welcome to learn alongside them.

Rabbis also had non-scholarly disciples. A century before Jesus, Rabbi Jose ben Joezer urged this type of follower to "Let your house be a gathering place for rabbis. Be covered in the dust of their feet. Drink in their words with enthusiasm".[5] In this context, being "covered in their dust" meant washing the dust off their feet when they visited your home. So the ideal non-scholarly disciple was someone who opened their home for scholars, met basic needs for them when they were there, and enjoyed listening to their discussions.

Only one disciple in the New Testament carries out these three duties perfectly – Mary, the sister of Martha. Both sisters welcomed Jesus into their house regularly and they were both hospitable. But Mary, unlike Martha, was also commended for spending time learning at Jesus' feet, while her sister reprimanded her for doing this (Luke 10:39–42). And Mary is even portrayed as an extravagantly diligent foot-washer, in contrast to the twelve who were famously reluctant to wash each other's feet at the Last Supper (John 12:1–8; 13:3–16). So the only person described as carrying out all three functions of a non-scholarly disciple in the Gospels is female! Significantly, she rather puts the other disciples to shame.

The point at which Jesus' disciples do shine is when they hit rock bottom. Peter's greatest moment occurred after his cowardice made him disown Jesus. When Jesus poignantly looked at him after his denials, Peter didn't respond with bluster or even self-loathing – he repented with tears of contrition. Similarly, when the disciples realized that Jesus really had risen from the dead, they didn't pretend they'd always known that. They were genuinely surprised and overjoyed. This was the quality which Jesus looked for in all his disciples – a willingness to learn and change. Jesus didn't require a flawless past or innate talents that promised a bright future. He looked for a willingness to change direction and follow faithfully.

Stories about other Jewish rabbis are very different from the Gospel accounts about the disciples. Rather like the later stories of Christian saints, we hear about the rabbis' scholarly prowess, their dedication to studying and obeying every detail of the law, and the wonderful ways in which they benefited the community. We never hear anything remotely bad or boring about them. In contrast, the Gospel stories are more like home movies than epic films: they show disciples who were fallible – making stupid mistakes, naive and simply not understanding who Jesus was or what he was teaching.

Jesus' disciples followed a different agenda to the disciples of other Jewish rabbis. They didn't care about their own reputation or greatness; they wanted only to tell the world about their rabbi Jesus. They learned this humility from Jesus himself who refused the honour due to masters and said: "Let no one call you rabbi or father or master" (Matthew 23:8–12). He lived among his disciples as an equal, even washing their feet.

When the disciples learned later that the authority of their master was literally out of this world, they must have felt so embarrassed about some of the ways they'd behaved, but they did nothing to cover this up. They faithfully made sure that everything their master taught and everything that had happened – even the things that reflected scandalously on them – was truthfully passed on and recorded.

When I look round in church on Sunday morning, I could easily think: What a bunch of losers we are! And I'm sure that's the same for all church groups because Christians tend to get to know each other very well. Our private lives, failures and embarrassments are often shared in prayer requests, testimonies, house group discussions, or general chats – all with an emphasis on honesty that is rare elsewhere. But my friends and I aren't losers; we're simply real, honest humans who don't always succeed, just like Jesus' disciples. The disciples Jesus wanted were *ordinary* people. When Paul looked round the church at Corinth he asked rhetorically: "Are there many wise or great among you?"

(1 Corinthians 1:20–31). Of course not! And the same should be true in all churches.

Jesus' disciples show us that it doesn't matter when we mess up, forget things, or do things for the wrong motives, so long as we turn round, say sorry to God and those we have hurt, and try to make things right. Sadly, people are often put off the Kingdom because of foolish or sinful Christians, but they shouldn't be. Customers shouldn't judge a product by its salesmen, and salesmen shouldn't take themselves too seriously. In the end, it's not about us; Jesus' disciples need only point to him.

Notes

1. Mishnah Ketubbot 5.6.
2. Babylonian Talmud Berakhot 62a.
3. Babylonian Talmud Hagigah 9b.
4. This is seen clearly at Jerusalem Talmud Sanhedrin 1.2 but also occurs at Babylonian Talmud Baba Batra 115b; Babylonian Talmud Menachot 65ab; Megillat Ta'anit 338.
5. Mishnah Abot 1.4.

The Unchosen

William Carey, the founder of the modern missionary movement at the end of the 1700s, was a heretic according to many in his denomination. Most Particular Baptist ministers were hyper-Calvinists who didn't believe in evangelism. They thought that God chooses certain people who will inevitably become Christians, and that Christ's death saves only them and no one else. This meant that evangelistic preaching was not only unnecessary, but might even be dangerous, because someone who was not chosen by God might repent! To make it worse, Carey wanted to reach heathen foreigners, which they considered even more dangerous because surely God hadn't chosen them! Fortunately, his pastor, Andrew Fuller, was a progressive thinker who wrote a book to combat the hyper-Calvinists' attitude to evangelism: *The Gospel Worthy of All Acceptation*. This argued that God wants the Gospel presented to everyone. Together, Carey and Fuller saved the English Baptists from stagnation and started a mission that now encircles the globe.

Many people in Jesus' day thought like Carey's critics. Thanks to the discoveries of the Qumran or Dead Sea Scrolls, we now know much more about the secretive community of Jews living at Qumran. They regarded themselves as the only ones who obeyed God's law properly and thought they had discovered hidden truths about the correct dates for festivals and the right way to worship God. They believed themselves to be the "Sons of Light", whom God would reward, whereas other people were "Sons of Darkness" whom God would punish. They had an abhorrent policy towards outsiders: they were commanded *not* to tell anyone about how to please God in case they, too, would be saved from destruction.[1] The Qumran Jews also believed that God keeps total control over whom he saves and that he chooses just a few (i.e. those in their community) and rejects the "many" whom he actually causes to follow a life a sin.[2]

The Pharisees, by contrast, believed that each person has a free choice about whether or not to follow God. They believed that all Jews would be saved, though those who followed the law perfectly would get higher honour. Rabbi Johanan ben Zakkai told a parable to illustrate this: A king summoned his servants to a banquet without appointing a time. The wise ones adorned themselves and waited in readiness at the door of the palace, but the fools went about their work. Suddenly the king announced that the banquet had begun and called in his servants. The wise entered suitably adorned, while the fools entered with soiled clothes. The king rejoiced at the wise, but was angry with the fools. He ordered: "Those who adorned themselves for the banquet can sit, eat and drink. But those who did not adorn themselves for the banquet, must stand and watch."[3]

As Johanan lived in Galilee at the same time as Jesus, Jesus probably heard him tell this parable and there are striking similarities with Jesus' own parables – those of the banquet, the wedding feast, and the wise and foolish virgins. But there are also significant differences. In Johanan's parable, everyone was invited and everyone was let in, though the fools suffered dishonour. Jesus, however, says in his parables that some missed out completely because of the choices they made: the foolish virgins didn't get ready and found the door shut (Matthew 25:10); the man who didn't dress properly was thrown out (Matthew 22:11–13); and those who didn't want to come and made excuses didn't get a second invitation (Luke 14:24).

In Jesus' parable of a banquet the first group of people with special invitations turned them down, saying that they had better things to do. The king then sent his servants to fetch everyone they could find in the streets – even to drag them in if they were hesitant. The banquet ended up being full – not with the special people who had received an invitation, but with the ordinary people who, though not originally on the official guest list, agreed to come nevertheless. This story is especially scandalous because Jesus took pains to highlight that surprising twist. For him, the crux of the story wasn't about the few "special" ones who refused to come, but about the many ordinary people who chose to come when they were given the opportunity.

Jesus summed up his parable with a strange slogan: "Many are called, but few are chosen" (Matthew 22:14). It's strange because in the story it was actually the other way round – originally it was just a few who were called or invited. And the many who came weren't "chosen" as the guests with proper invitations had been – they "chose" to come when the doors were open. It's as if Jesus wanted to emphasize his disagreement with Qumran beliefs. They dismissed everyone else (the "many") as "Sons of Darkness" who were rejected by God, and said that only a few Jews were actually the "chosen" ones. But Jesus said the "many" were *called* by God, though most of them decided not to come. And although Qumran interpreted the word "chosen" to mean that we don't have a choice, Jesus said in this parable that we *do* have a choice – though it also hints that God sometimes pushes us hard to persuade us.

Jesus implied in these parables that people choose to follow God. It wasn't because they were too poor or ignorant that the virgins didn't have enough oil in their lamps – they foolishly decided not to bother, just like the guest who didn't bother to dress properly or the others who couldn't be bothered to attend. Jesus' other parables indicate that this choice is often made difficult – the parable of the sower said that materialism and spiritual evil can impede us. Perhaps that's why the servants were told to help some people accept the invitation by dragging them inside!

For Jesus, evangelism was important because he taught that everyone has to accept God's invitation, and that some need a friendly push to help them. Today we shy away from evangelism and instead wait for people to make up their own minds. This sounds laudable until we think of it in terms of Jesus' parable: it's equivalent to hoarding a pile of invitations and not giving them out unless someone comes and asks us for one. Our polite reticence can mean that we don't actually invite anyone into God's Kingdom, but Jesus' message is clear – we need to give everyone that choice.

Notes

1. *Rule of the Community* 9:17.
2. *Damascus Document* 2.13–17.
3. Babylonian Talmud Shabbat 153a.

The Cursed

I had no idea my friend's sister had AIDS until I casually asked one day how his family was. He told me the terrible news that his sister had died the day before. His family back in Zimbabwe had found it increasingly impossible to get the medication which had been keeping his vivacious and happy sister in good health. He told me that he had discovered that she'd contracted it from infected blood after a routine operation, but people had made the assumption that it was a "lifestyle" illness. Sadly, the judgmentalism of some had meant that, as well as being a cause of great sorrow for her and her family, the illness had also been a cause of shame.

Scandal was associated with most types of illness in the ancient world, because health and disease were attributed directly to God as a gift or punishment. For example, in Judaism it was thought that jaundice was due to hating someone without reason; respiratory illnesses such as asthma were caused by slandering someone or neglecting to pay your tithes; while oedema (usually caused by high blood pressure) was due to sin in general.[1]

The Jews also thought that the Old Testament punishment of being "cut off from the people", which was prescribed for various sins, had been carried out by God if someone had a fatal illness before the age of fifty. So anyone who fell ill and died was assumed to have a scandalous sin in their past which God had punished, and the earlier they died, the more serious their sin had been.

They even thought that someone with disabilities was being

punished. This was based on the Old Testament law that said that anyone with congenital defects or disabilities shouldn't enter the Temple (Leviticus 21:17–21). In its original context, this law concerned the priests who served in the Temple and it can be seen as a way to excuse disabled priests from carrying out their duties there. But the Jews in New Testament times applied it to everyone and this resulted in disabled people being forbidden from worshipping in the Temple. "Unclean" people, such as lepers and menstruating women, were also kept away (this was probably due to the misguided widespread fear of contamination, which could have caused chaos in a crowded environment like the Temple). These regulations implied that God shunned such people, so they reinforced the idea that disability and illness were due to sin.

The Jewish community of Qumran was even stricter. They wouldn't let anyone join them if they were blind, handicapped, blemished or emasculated, and they even excluded "doddery old men unable to do their share in the community".[2] This rule was also based on the Old Testament law about handicapped priests, from which they mistakenly concluded that handicapped people weren't as holy as others. It resulted in them not wanting to "contaminate" the community with such people.

Jesus surprised everyone by his refusal to avoid lepers, the blind, the lame or anyone else who was sick and, by doing so, he could not have emphasized more clearly that he believed the complete opposite about illness and disability. His followers still assumed that Jesus wouldn't want to meet ill or disabled people and tried to stop them reaching him: the crowd wouldn't make way for the paralysed man, so his friends had to resort to lowering him through the roof to see Jesus (Mark 10:46–48); and when some blind men shouted for Jesus, the people didn't help them and even tried to stop them calling to him (Luke 18:35–39).

This attitude explains why the woman with chronic menstrual problems sneaked up behind Jesus and secretly touched him (Luke 8:43–48) – she assumed that Jesus would want to avoid her.

Even birth defects in Jesus' day were ascribed to sin. Jesus' disciples asked him about a man who was blind from birth: "Was the sin committed by the man or his parents?" (John 9:2). Jesus said that the man's blindness had nothing to do with sin and demonstrated this by simply healing him without asking him about sin or repentance. On another occasion, Jesus did say, "Your sins are forgiven" before healing a paralysed man (Mark 2:5–12). However, he pointedly kept the matters of forgiveness and healing entirely separate – he didn't ask the man whether he had actually repented before healing him. Perhaps Jesus knew that the man was overwhelmed with feelings of inappropriate guilt, which is hardly surprising when everyone else believed his paralysis was due to sin of some kind.

Although Jesus never asked anyone to repent from their sins before he healed them and denied that a certain man's blindness was due to sin, this doesn't mean that sin and illness are never connected. Paul said that some of the believers at Corinth were ill because of their sinfulness (1 Corinthians 11:29–30) and modern medicine recognizes that intractable guilt can contribute to a variety of ill effects, from depression to physical weakness, and an impaired response to infections. David testified about the terrible physical effects he suffered when he refused to confess his sin: "Before I confessed, my bones wasted away and… my strength was sapped" (Psalm 32:3–5).

However, Jesus taught that illness due to sin is exceptional; he wanted to discourage his disciples and others from jumping to the widespread assumption that an ill person had a scandal in their past. Paul had feared that the believers in Galatia might assume God was punishing him when he arrived with an illness

– he expected them to treat him "with contempt or scorn", especially when he didn't get better. But, instead, he records how relieved he was when they received him as if he were "an angel from God" (Galatians 4:14). They had learned from Jesus' teaching.

Some churches today still teach that unanswered prayer for healing indicates a sin or lack of faith. However, Jesus did not require people to have faith before they were healed, though, of course, he encouraged people to have faith in God. When his disciples asked how much faith was needed, Jesus' reply cited the smallest measure of size available – a mustard seed. Nowadays he'd say: "Even an atom of faith is enough." Some of those whom Jesus healed had absolutely no faith – for example, the man who was born blind didn't even know who Jesus was (John 9:35–38) and no one had faith on his behalf because his carers denied faith in Jesus (John 9:18–22). He had no one to turn to but Jesus, and, in healing him, Jesus demonstrated that the smallness of someone's faith is unimportant next to the greatness of the God who heals us.

Some Bible verses appear to teach that God heals all illnesses, but we have to read them in their context. For example, Psalm 103:2–3 praises God whose benefits include forgiving all sin and healing all diseases. This sounds as though a believer should never die! When we read it in context, however, we find that this is a song of thanks that praises God as the one who forgives and heals – that is, it praises God as the one from whom all forgiveness comes, and from whom all healing ultimately comes. The word "benefits" in verse 2 can mislead us into thinking of welfare benefits or benefits in an insurance policy, but following God is not the same as buying insurance. When we are sick, we pray (i.e. ask) – we don't file a claim and demand our "benefits"! God loves us and, therefore, like any good parent, he doesn't take orders from his children because we don't always know what is best.

Christian commitment shines out as powerfully in the care of the sick as it does in their healing through Christian prayer. Former communist states such as Russia and Romania still discriminate against disabled people, and parents in those societies are often so ashamed of their disabled children that they put them into a state "orphanage". The ideal Christian community cares for the sick and prays for the sick. It has the faith to pray for healing, the faith to accept God's will if he doesn't heal – and the faith to praise God in either circumstance.

Notes

1. Babylonian Talmud Shabbat 33a – this was already a fixed tradition when Eleazar ben Rabbi Jose commented on it in the early second century.
2. Rule of the Congregation 2:7.

Prostitutes

One night a flasher sneaked through the grounds of Tyndale House where I work. He waited until a pretty young lady was sitting on her own at a desk facing the window and then exposed himself. He ended up humiliated. After the initial shock of seeing a face at the window, she looked at him and burst out laughing. He ran away hurriedly and she began to feel a bit sorry for him. He didn't know that she regularly did mission work among prostitutes and often had to confront their bosses; she was used to dealing with dangerous and seedy situations.

I imagine that Jesus was equally unshockable. Unlike the rest of his respectable generation, Jesus went out of his way to meet prostitutes; they were part of the humanity he came to save. The Pharisees were scandalized that he should accept invitations to eat with "tax collectors and sinners", but Jesus said: "It is the sick who need a physician, so I don't seek the righteous but the sinners" (Mark 2:17). This was a clever answer, but it didn't deal with the Pharisees' main problem: Jesus spending his time with sinners was bad enough, but they weren't just sinners – they were prostitutes. Prostitutes at that time were called "sinners" in polite company, just as they were called "fallen women" by the Victorians. Interestingly, the Gospels never record Jesus using a euphemism, so when he condemned the Pharisees he said: "Tax collectors and *prostitutes* will get to the Kingdom of heaven before you" (Matthew 21:31).

Why is it that "tax collectors" are linked so often with these "sinners" (i.e. "prostitutes")? And why are they usually mentioned in the context of Jesus eating with them? (See Matthew 9:10–11; 11:19; 21:31–32.) The reason is that Roman-style banquets usually included prostitutes for the after-dinner entertainment – lap dancing without any restrictions. And as tax collectors were the *nouveaux riches*, trying to keep up with the Roman fashions, of course they provided all the customary dining "facilities". Perhaps the woman who broke her alabaster perfume bottle over Jesus' feet had met him at one of these meals (Matthew 26:6–7).

Jesus wasn't soft on sin, but he understood sinners. He pointed out that fantasizing about a person was spiritually equivalent to acting out that fantasy because both acts are deliberate and one can lead to the other. In fact he said that inner filth can be worse than visible filth (Matthew 5:27–28; Mark 7:18–23). His emphasis on motives as well as actions doesn't mean that he downplayed the significance of sinful acts, but he wanted to point out to those who think they are righteous that they are actually sinners who need his help.

Jesus put his finger on the weak spot of the Pharisees – a common weakness which they were loath to admit. We quip that men think about sex every seven seconds and this may explain why the Pharisees were constantly concerned about preventing sexual thoughts. They went to extreme lengths such as avoiding touching their penis even while urinating[1] and trying hard not to even accidentally touch a woman. (Some said that touching a woman's little finger was as serious as touching her genitals.)[2] While walking down the street, they would stare at the ground to avoid seeing any women – some even boasted about the wounds they got from accidentally walking into walls![3] All this to avoid the temptation caused by women! But Jesus didn't put the blame on women; he pointed out that these thoughts come from within a person, not from outside.

Jesus sounds somewhat preoccupied with sex when he calls the new generation in Palestine "sinful and adulterous" (Mark 8:38) – especially as "sinful" in this context would refer to prostitutes. However, it was simply an accurate assessment of how his society had recently changed. Before the Roman army took over Judea in AD 6 there would have been few, if any, prostitutes in the very religious society of Palestine, but afterwards the presence of Roman soldiers created a demand for them. Paradoxically, this was because the soldiers were so disciplined – unlike other armies, they weren't allowed to rape or even to get married, so they were forced to pay for sex.

Some soldiers did, in fact, find a way round these regulations by creating a novel form of marriage certificate that was disguised as a loan certificate. Several of these have been found by archaeologists and they record a "loan" made by a soldier to a woman without any repayment terms. It was similar to a marriage certificate which records gifts to the bride, though without the marriage vows. When the soldiers retired, they could declare their "marriage" publicly. However, this ingenious way of getting married was merely a heart-warming exception; most soldiers turned to prostitutes, and many poor people and former slaves fell into the profession as a result.

We can sympathize with these soldiers and prostitutes without condoning their actions. It is striking that the Old Testament doesn't actually condemn ordinary prostitutes, though it utterly condemns cultic prostitutes who had sex with "worshippers" at temples of the old Canaanite gods (Deuteronomy 23:17; Jeremiah 2:20). Also, there is severe condemnation for those who make people into prostitutes (Leviticus 19:29) and criticism of those who use them (Genesis 38; Proverbs 23:27; 29:3). Prostitutes themselves, however, were not ostracized by society – they could own property and could even present legal cases before the highest court of the land (1 Kings 3:16–27).

The book of Proverbs regards adultery as a far worse sin than an unmarried man turning to a prostitute (Proverbs 7:5–21). It regards both as wrong, though it points out that "a prostitute only wants a loaf of bread, but an adulteress hunts you for your precious soul" (Proverbs 6:26). Interestingly, many modern Bibles consider this is too soft on prostitutes, so they translate it as "a prostitute leaves you with nothing but a loaf of bread…"

Jesus was sympathetic to the individuals without being soft on the sin itself. When asked to affirm the death penalty for a woman "caught in the act", he asked for those without sin to throw the first stone. It was only after everyone else had searched their hearts and left that he got tough with her: he told her to stop sinning (John 8:11). If she was a prostitute this meant that he was also telling her, in effect, to become unemployed with no prospect that anyone else would employ her.[4]

The Bible shows us that prostitutes can be rehabilitated, marry and even become highly respected, though they may face severe prejudice. The law allowed a former prostitute to marry just like everyone else, though she couldn't marry a priest. This wasn't on moral grounds – as if prostitution was beyond the pale – because priests were also forbidden to marry divorcees and widows. The most important family tree in the Bible – that of the Messiah – contains two prostitutes: Tamar, who became pregnant while pretending to be a full-time prostitute; and Rahab (Matthew 1:3, 5; Genesis 38; Joshua 6:25). Some commentators are embarrassed by this and have tried to redefine Rahab as an "innkeeper", but the text unambiguously calls her a "prostitute" (*zonah* in Hebrew).

The early church contained former sex workers and their clients, as Paul points out to the Corinthians (1 Corinthians 6:9–11), but to how many churches today could Paul say, "And that is what some of you were"? Maybe this is because most churches have done very little work among this group, though fortunately this is now changing. The organization Stop The Traffik is a prime example – it has linked together different charities and organizations who are working in this field and campaigns against modern slavery and sex traffic. Steve Chalke, one of its founders, has been appointed the UN Special Advisor on Community Action against Human Trafficking, which is a wonderful official recognition of the work done by churches and others in this area.

How many Christians work among the street walkers in their own church locality? Unlike Jesus, who accepted invitations to meals where prostitutes would be present, we tend to avoid any situations which might even appear salacious or compromising to our reputation. Prime Minister William Gladstone, who had a great deal to lose if his reputation was sullied, chose to ignore this danger. He set up and personally worked in charities which helped prostitutes leave that profession. Similar problems may face such workers today, but whatever reasons churches give for not helping those caught up in the sex industry, Jesus' example shows us that we should think again.

Notes

1. Mishnah Niddah 2.1; Babylonian Talmud Niddah 13a–b.
2. Babylonian Talmud Shabbat 1.9.
3. Babylonian Talmud Sotah 22b.
4. This story is dismissed by some historians because it is missing from many of the early Gospel manuscripts. However, rather than a later generation making up the story, it is more likely that people in the early church censored it from their own copy of the Gospel to prevent women in their family thinking that adultery wasn't serious. Although the Jews had lost the right to carry out capital punishment, stoning by a mob could still occur, and zealots were known to kill someone without trial in the Temple area, where this incident occurred (John 18:31; Acts 7:57–58; Mishnah Sanhedrin 9.6). See Roger Aus, *Caught in the Act: Walking on the Sea and the Release of Barabbas Revisited*, Atlanta: Scholars, 1998, especially pp. 1–26.

PART 3

SCANDALS IN JESUS' TEACHING

Child Abuse

The Mafia terrorized New York during the Prohibition years by letting everyone know the punishment for informants – the so-called "concrete shoes". Victims were stood in quick-drying cement, then dropped overboard in the Hudson River. They probably didn't carry this out quite as often as the movies suggest, however – they didn't need to!

Jesus issued an even worse threat when he said of a group of people: "It would have been better for them if they'd had a millstone hung round their neck and had been dropped into the sea" (Matthew 18:6; Mark 9:42). He tells this group that their actual punishment would be far worse – something that would make them wish they'd had this lesser punishment instead. The fury in the warning is unmistakable.

Who is this chilling anger directed at? Jesus issued this extraordinary threat just after he had taken a small child in his arms to teach his disciples about humility. When he finished the lesson, he looked at the child and described this terrible fate for anyone who "causes one of these little ones to stumble" (*skandalizo* in Greek).

What does Jesus mean by "stumble"? *Skandalizo* can be translated as anything from "causing offence" to "causing sin", which in the Gospels and Jewish Greek literature usually refers to sexual sin. All kinds of sexual sins and temptations were referred to using the word "stumble". In two popular Jewish works written a couple of centuries before Jesus, young men were warned not to "gaze at a virgin, lest her beauty makes you stumble" and to avoid "the wicked woman who will make you stumble".[1] In the Sermon on the Mount, Jesus warns against "looking at a woman lustfully" and immediately afterwards warns that your "eye" or your "hand" might cause you to stumble (Matthew 5:28–30). This language is clearly euphemistic, though it was more obvious for ancient Jews because the Hebrew word for "hand" also meant "penis".

Jesus follows his warning about sinning with children by a similar warning about an eye or hand which could lead people into sin (Matthew 18:6–8; Mark 9:42–43). His language might be euphemistic (there was a child present!), but the implication is obvious. Jesus is talking about child sex abuse, which he hated with more ferocity than he expressed for any other sin.

Sadly, such abuse was very common in Roman society and when their armies occupied Palestine, they brought this curse with them. Plautus (a playwright who lived in about 200 BC) summarized Roman sexual morals as: "you can make love to anything you like, so long as you keep away from wives, widows, virgins, young men and free-born boys".[2] The gaps in this list – that is, those with whom fornication was supposedly OK – were professional women such as prostitutes and actresses, loose women, and slave girls or boys. Pretty boys were sold at a high price because a "diligent" host needed young boys to be waiters or even nude dancers and, as slaves, they were not permitted to repel sexual advances by the guests.

Some upper-class Jews began to be corrupted by Roman customs. Philo, a Jew from first-century Egypt, said fellow Jews were emulating Roman banquets by providing all kinds of "luxuries" including "slaves of the utmost comeliness and beauty, giving the idea that they have come not so much to render service as to give pleasure... Some just beginning to show a beard on their youthful chins, having been, for a short time, the sport of the profligate debauchees, and being prepared with exceeding care and diligence for more painful services".[3]

A picture of this kind of social event is preserved for us on the side of a silver wine cup – the Warren Cup – which is exhibited in the British Museum. It shows two scenes of homoerotic activity: one scene where an older man is penetrating a young man and a similar scene with two young boys who have not yet cut off their adolescent long hair (which was usually done at age sixteen). A small detail is perhaps the most poignant – there is a little slave boy looking anxiously into the room round the door he has just opened. He has either glimpsed something he shouldn't have or, more likely, he has been called to "service" a guest and is horrified at what he sees going on. He looks as if he is about ten years old. The model for the artist could have been a playmate of Jesus, because this cup was made in about AD 10 and was found in Bittir, near Bethlehem.

The Romans brought more than just the horrors of war to Palestine: they brought their immoral lifestyle and oppressive slavery. Although Jews had slaves as well, their law gave slaves almost the same rights as free members of the household. But in Roman law, a slave was merely property, so owners could beat them to death or use them as a sex toy in any way they wished.

One of the reasons that child sex abuse is such a horrific crime is because of its long-term consequences. When a child is sexually abused they often have problems forming normal relationships or even trusting anyone for the rest of their lives. If they are abused at an early age, they feel personally guilty and sinful – feelings which are almost impossible to remove even when they realize the truth as adults. They can continue to suffer for the rest of their lives.

Judaism wasn't totally free of such vices. They recognized that some individuals had these temptations and guarded against them. There was a rule, for example, that unmarried men were not allowed to teach children unaccompanied.[4] If only the church had adopted that rule!

Child sex abuse is today rightly condemned by all societies, and those who try to cover up such abuse are equally condemned. Jesus spoke out against this practice with more vehemence than anyone else of his day, and the Gospels record him speaking more stridently against this than anything else. Our society and the church have only recently learned to view this crime with as much seriousness as Jesus.

Notes

1. Sirach 9:5; Psalms of Solomon 32:15.
2. *Curvulio* 37–38.
3. Philo, *Contemplative Life* 6, 48–52.
4. Mishnah Qiddushin 4.13.

Hypocrisy

A church I know is dying from hypocrisy. And although I'm watching it from a distance, it's still painful. The congregation is small, though very faithful, and the minister is a natural evangelist. But whenever someone is converted through an Alpha course or pub ministry they don't stay in the church for long. The members soon show them that they are inadequate for their new faith: these new believers know nothing about the depth and traditions of Christianity; they fumble their way round the Bible and Prayer Book; they don't have the gravitas or decorum for respectful worship; and those who have children, can't control them properly. The old faithful, who are becoming fewer in number, can't understand why the new believers don't make more effort to be like them and to support the church like they do. They can't see that they are suffering from that peculiar form of hypocrisy identified by Jesus – doing all the "right" things for all the wrong reasons. And this results in repelling people from God.

I feel sorry for the Pharisees of Jesus' day. I spend a lot of time reading their writings and many of them are like friends to me. They sincerely tried to obey all of God's commandments and yet the Gospels portray them as enemies, and Jesus spends a lot of time accusing them of hypocrisy (e.g. see Matthew 23). The Greek word *hupokritēs* was the technical word for an actor, so Jesus was criticizing them for "pretending" or "play-acting". Perhaps this doesn't seem a very serious charge, but Jesus pointed out that in behaving this way the Pharisees were making it difficult for others to follow God. Their aim was to follow God's law to the letter, and to do this they created many other laws which defined ever so carefully what they thought God's law said. There were so many new religious laws that ordinary people had no hope of keeping them all unless they had the leisure to spend their lives studying how to carry them out.

Many of the new laws didn't affect the religious leaders who created them. For example, in their six-volume law collection called the *Mishnah*, the first volume was mostly devoted to religious laws concerning farming. The Pharisees had lost sight of what the law was all about, and for the common people, these extra laws became a huge burden of guilt. Jesus, in contrast, regarded only the Old Testament laws as God-given guidelines for life. He criticized these pharisaic laws as being unscriptural – a huge and unnecessary expansion of Old Testament law.

Why did the Gospel writers spend so much time telling us about the Pharisees? Perhaps because of what happened when a group of them found their way into the new-born church. A contingent of Pharisees became Christians while remaining practising Pharisees. There was nothing necessarily wrong with this. Jews who became Christians didn't have to stop being Jews – they had found their Messiah and they could worship Jesus in the Temple and in synagogues as some of the apostles did. In the same way, the Christian Pharisees were allowed to carry on following their extra rules. The problem came when they demanded that *all* Christians should also obey these rules.

The scandal of hypocrisy started to become endemic in the church. The Pharisees' legal mindset and Scripture knowledge made them natural teachers, so they had a huge influence on many of the recently formed congregations and even on the leadership. In time, even the top leaders in the church were influenced by them. Paul publicly accused some fellow Christian leaders of this kind of hypocrisy themselves – including his mentor Barnabas and the apostle Peter!

Although there probably weren't many Pharisees in the early church, those few had a big effect. The first church council was called because some of them demanded that all Gentile Christians should be circumcised (Acts 15:5), and two of Paul's letters (Galatians and Romans) grapple with this issue. Peter notably stood up to this "Circumcision Party" when they criticized him for eating with Gentiles – even though they'd seen those same Gentiles filled with the Holy Spirit (see Acts 10:45; 11:2). But sometimes even Peter followed the Pharisaic restrictions. When he went to Antioch to meet the new Gentile converts there, he was happy to eat with them. However, as soon as some of the "Circumcision Party" turned up, he switched back to eating only with Jews. That's when Paul publicly called Peter a hypocrite (Galatians 2:11–13).

It would be a mistake to say that all Pharisees were hypocrites but they themselves recognized it as a problem within their movement. A second-century Jewish saying lists seven ways in which Pharisees obeyed religious laws for the wrong motives. Five of these could be classed as hypocrisy: obeying the laws simply to look good; being proud of your humility; avoiding temptation in a publicly exaggerated way; making sure people saw your fatigue and misery from fasting; and asking advice about religious matters so that you could show off how much you already knew. This saying also listed two other wrong motives for obeying religious laws: obeying them out of fear and obeying them out of love. They regarded love of God as a *bad* motive for obedience, because they said that religious laws should be obeyed simply because they were laws from God.

Jesus taught the opposite. He said that the whole purpose of the laws given in the Bible is to promote love – love for God and love for people (Matthew 22:37–40). Their purpose is to help us live closer to God and in harmony with our neighbours – not to trip us up and make us into miserable sinners. But for many Pharisees – who were known as "pestle Pharisees" because they walked around with exaggeratedly bowed heads, like the bent handle of an ancient pestle – misery was equated with piety.

Jesus enjoyed life too much, according to the Pharisees. I love the way he is portrayed in *The Miracle Maker*, a film by Murray Watts. Although this Jesus is made of coloured clay, he is more lifelike than some actors. And, unlike most other portrayals, he is often seen to be laughing. This matches the portrayal of Jesus in the Gospels where we see him attending several parties, making vast quantities of wine for a wedding, telling amusing stories and being criticized by the Pharisees for never organizing a fast (Matthew 9:14). Jesus didn't deny that he was a party lover. He loved people and wanted to be wherever they were. Jesus kept the Old Testament law perfectly, but this didn't make him anti-social like many of the Pharisees.

Our churches still contain hypocrites and few of us escape being one of them at some time. We do all the right things, but often for very dubious motives. We criticize those whose spirituality is different: they cling to tradition or they want too much change; they are too "buttoned up" during worship or they are too emotional; they have messed-up lives or they are too successful. The Pharisee side of us comes out especially when we make church rules, because most church rules define who is in and who is out. When we make rules – whether they are written ones or not – we must ask the question that governed Jesus' attitude: Does this rule help us to love God and love our neighbour more? The scandal in the early church was that the Pharisees felt so at home. This is one way in which we *don't* want to emulate the early church.

Polygamy

I'm sure you've heard this question before – it's a favourite of those who like to harry unsuspecting church leaders: When a polygamous African tribal chief converts to Christianity, what happens to all his wives? Should he divorce them and send them back to their parents' homes in shame and penury, or should he live away from them in a separate house but continue to provide for them financially? This is a classic problem for missionaries in countries that practise polygamy and one to which there is no easy answer... just the fervent hope that the next generation will marry only one wife! It must seem very strange for those polygamous families, when their normal, socially acceptable lifestyle is suddenly regarded as scandalously immoral.

The Jews whom Jesus lived among had the same problem. Polygamy had been considered perfectly normal and proper until the Romans took over and said it was disgusting and immoral. By Jesus' time, many Jews had come to agree with the Roman view and polygamy fell out of practice during subsequent generations, although the Jews did not actually outlaw polygamy until the eleventh century. (It was rather like slave ownership in the UK not being practised for years, but not actually being made officially illegal until 2009 simply because legislators hadn't got round to it.)[1]

The Romans allowed Jews to continue practising polygamy in Palestine, but elsewhere in the Empire monogamy was strictly enforced. Many Jews living outside Palestine therefore got used to the principle of having one wife and it seemed natural to them. We don't know how frequent polygamy was among the Jews in Palestine because we have the complete family records of only one family, dating from the early second century – the papyrus scrolls were preserved in a bag hidden in a desert cave. They include the marriage certificate of a widow called Babatha who married a man who already had a wife. Babatha owned her own land and business, so she didn't marry for financial support – perhaps it was for companionship or even love.

The Old Testament allowed polygamy but didn't encourage it. Great men like Abraham, Israel, Judah, Gideon, Samson, David and Solomon had multiple wives, though the Old Testament records many problems which resulted. However, the law actually made it mandatory in one circumstance: if a married man died without leaving a male heir, his brother was required to marry the widow, whether or not he already had a wife. This was so that she would have support during her old age (either from her new husband or from her son) and so that the family name and land would be passed on. Polygamy was also allowed in other circumstances, presumably for similarly practical reasons such as the reduced number of men available for marriage after a war. This not only helped women who would otherwise be on their own, but also helped to replace the population more quickly. In peacetime, however, this practice meant that rich men had more than one wife and poor men remained single.

Jesus took the side of the Romans against the Jewish establishment on this occasion. Most Jews outside Palestine and some in Palestine also stood out against polygamy – for example, the Qumran sect. They regarded it as one of the three most scandalous sins (called "the nets of the devil") by which the "smooth-speaking" Pharisees entrapped the people (they didn't like the Pharisees!).[2]

The Qumran sect couldn't actually find a single verse in the Old Testament from which to teach this, so they combined two different verses to support this doctrine. They found two verses with the same phrase – "male and female" – in Genesis 1:27 and 7:9. The first says, "God created them male and female" and the second says, "They went into the ark, two by two, male and female". Since "male and female" meant "two" in chapter 7, they inferred that it also meant "two" in chapter 1 and concluded from this that only two people could marry. They referred to this doctrine as "the foundation of creation". We may not be convinced by their logic, but as far as they were concerned it was case proven.

Jews outside Palestine used a different verse to show that polygamy was wrong – Genesis 2:24: "a man shall… be joined to his wife" – which implies one man and one wife. To emphasize this conclusion, they added the word "two" to the second part of the original Hebrew sentence as follows: "and those *two* shall become one flesh". We find this word added to the text in all ancient translations of the Hebrew – in Greek, Aramaic, Syriac and even Samaritan – showing that it had widespread support. Presumably it also had some support among Hebrew speakers, but no one in Jesus' day would deliberately change the original Hebrew text.

When the Pharisees were questioning Jesus about divorce he took the opportunity to set them straight about polygamy, using both sets of arguments. He quoted the key verse used by the Qumran Jews (Genesis 1:27) and even said this was what happened "at the beginning of creation" (Mark 10:6, which presumably reminded his listeners of the Qumran "foundation of creation"). Then he quoted the verse preferred by Jews outside Palestine – Genesis 2:24 – including the additional word "two" (Mark 10:8; Matthew 19:5). By deliberately using both arguments, Jesus' emphasis on monogamy was very clear to his listeners.

Paul took the teaching against polygamy further by reversing the command that a man had to marry his dead brother's wife. This had always been a difficult rule, though it made sense in the world of the early Old Testament. In Hittite law (and probably other Ancient Near Eastern laws) a widow could be married against her will to any male relative – even to her husband's grandfather, but Moses' law restricted this to someone of roughly her age (i.e. only a brother of her husband) and allowed her to refuse. Now, Paul decided that it was outmoded because few Jews still had family land, so there was not the necessity to ensure a new generation to pass it on to. He said that a widow could marry whoever she wanted (1 Corinthians 7:39).

Enforcing monogamy may have cleared away a scandal, but it created a new problem for the church. Suddenly there were more widows without husbands and without support because they couldn't become anyone's second wife. To try to help these widows the church created a new type of social club for them. This spread outside Palestine as a good solution to a problem which had always existed there because polygamy was not allowed. It was one of the first things the fledgling church did, and right from the start it was problematic – Greek-speaking widows complained that the Aramaic speakers were being given more food, for one thing (Acts 6:1). Young Timothy, leading the church in Ephesus, had other problems with his widows' group and Paul had to write a whole chapter to help him cope (1 Timothy 5). Nevertheless the club was a good solution to their needs and it was far better than the scandal that was caused by polygamy.

Why did Jesus and Paul change God's commands? Had God's first intention always been for monogamy and were they now going back to his original wishes? Although Jesus did say that this was how things were at the "beginning", it doesn't mean that God had subsequently given the wrong commands to Moses. It was the *purpose* of these commands, rather than the commands themselves that was important. And it was God's purpose that Jesus and Paul were upholding.

God's purpose for marriage was to help individuals find mutual support in families. When there were too few men (due to warfare) this purpose was accomplished by allowing polygamy to ensure male heirs. In more stable times, polygamy resulted in many men remaining single – the rich caused an imbalance because wealthy men could have many wives. In order to maintain God's purposes at times like these, the rule about polygamy had to change. God's purposes are eternal but his commands change in order to carry out those purposes in different situations.

We can feel smug that our society doesn't allow polygamy, but in some ways we are like the Romans, whose law was based on a morality that most didn't follow. Despite their official condemnation of polygamy, many "respectable" Romans had multiple marriages and multiple mistresses. Divorce was common and easily obtained (see the chapter "No-fault Divorce"). Eurydice, a newly wed Roman wife in the first century, was given advice about a happy marriage by Plutarch which included: "If your husband commit some peccadillo with a paramour or a maidservant, you ought not to be indignant or angry, because it is respect for you which leads him to share his debauchery, licentiousness, and wantonness with another woman."[3] In other words, adultery was so normal that she shouldn't take offence.

In modern Western societies, various surveys have revealed that 20–50 per cent of women and 30–60 per cent of men commit adultery – and this is something which is likely to be *under*-reported by those who are questioned. Perhaps soap operas don't misrepresent such scandals in our society as much as we would like to believe they do.

Jesus criticized polygamy as a warped version of the lifelong committed relationship of a one-plus-one marriage. Our society recognizes that this is a very special relationship, and we strive towards it, but in many cases we fail. So much time and money is often spent on the wedding and an almost equal amount on a subsequent divorce, but little time, care and attention is given to the marriage itself. Christian organizations such as Care for the Family help to correct that imbalance by working with couples who want to keep that extra-special relationship healthy, strong – and strictly one-to-one!

Notes

1. Section 71 of the Coroners and Justice Act 2009 created a new offence of holding another person in slavery or servitude or requiring them to perform forced or compulsory labour, because prior to this there was no single offence that fully covered the crime. See www.bbc.co.uk/news/uk-1488811.
2. Damascus Scroll 5.
3. *Coniugalia Praecepta* 16.

No-fault Divorce

I come from Brighton, which, in my childhood, was a popular destination for illicit lovers going away for a "dirty weekend". In those days it gave Brighton a rather risqué reputation. It also meant that a large number of private investigators operated in the town, hired to catch adulterers. As a child I had a perverse pride when I read yet another newspaper story about a divorce case citing a liaison in Brighton.

Paradoxically, the private investigator was often hired by the man he was supposedly investigating. He'd be given the name of a hotel, a room number and be instructed to turn up "unexpectedly" at a certain time. The man would hire a prostitute to sit in bed with him and call for room service at the pre-arranged time. When the maid brought the food she would see them both in bed and the investigator would slip in behind her armed with a camera. This provided two witnesses and photographic proof that could be used in the divorce case.

Fabricating evidence of your own infidelity was one of the easiest ways you could get a divorce, as it was very difficult to obtain one for any reason except adultery. But in 1969 divorce legislation was revolutionized on both sides of the Atlantic. In the UK, the Divorce Reform Act allowed divorce for anything considered to be "unreasonable behaviour" which led to the "irretrievable breakdown" of the marriage. In the USA, Governor Reagan signed a divorce bill that made California the first state to introduce no-fault divorce; this eventually spread to every other state in the nation. Previously, in both countries, only the wronged partner could file for a divorce and it was only allowed for a specific set of grounds; now, even an innocent partner could be divorced against their will.

This significant change in divorce legislation was very similar to the scandal that was happening when Jesus was going about his ministry. The Old Testament allowed divorce for adultery and for neglect (see the chapter "Marital Abuse"), but just before Jesus' day the rabbis introduced a new type of divorce called the "Any Cause" divorce. This allowed a man to divorce a woman for any cause whatsoever. Scandalous examples include a single burnt meal in one case and, in another, a wrinkle on his wife's face that she didn't have when he married her![1]. Divorces like these – for "Any Cause" – were, in effect, what we call today no-fault divorces. The reasons given for this type of divorce could be extremely minor and were therefore completely different to the Old Testament laws for divorce which the Jews still cited in their marriage contracts.

Every married Jew in Jesus' day had a marriage contract – some of these have been found in caves around the Dead Sea. They recorded the marriage vows made by the partners, listed the money and goods they both brought into the household, and detailed how much both of them would lose if they didn't keep their vows. English translations of the Bible tend to use the word "covenant" instead of the word "contract" for the Hebrew word *berith* (see Proverbs 2:1,17; Malachi 2:14) because "contract" makes marriage sound too "business-like". However, not using the word "contract" has the effect of blurring what was a very important element: the penalties for the marriage vows being broken.

Only one covenant in the Bible has no penalties – the wonderfully exceptional "new covenant" that God promised his people (Jeremiah 31:31). All the other covenants in the Bible have stipulations, with penalties if they aren't carried out, just like modern business contracts. The vows and divorce settlements of biblical marriage contracts are just as serious as the "blessings and curses" of treaty contracts (e.g. Deuteronomy 27–30) and the stipulations and penalties of business contracts.

The penalties prescribed for breaking marriage vows were mainly financial. In Jewish marriages just before Jesus' day, the groom promised that if he broke his vows he would return the dowry money plus a minimum of 200 *zuz* (about £20,000 or $30,000 in our money), so a poor person couldn't afford to get divorced. If the bride broke her vows her husband would retain the dowry when they divorced.

If a marriage vow was broken by one of the parties, it didn't mean that divorce was compulsory; the wronged partner could decide whether to forgive or to divorce. However, in Jesus day, some rabbis were starting to teach that divorce *was* compulsory for adultery. Jesus reminded them that Moses didn't "command" divorce; he merely "allowed" it (Matthew 19:7–8). Jesus encouraged the wronged partner to forgive their spouse for the broken vows, though he didn't say how many times.

Many of the prophets envisioned Israel's relationship with God as a marriage covenant, where God was a jealous and long-suffering husband and Israel was an adulterous wife who worshipped other gods. God eventually decided to "divorce" Israel by sending her into exile, and threatened to do the same to the sister nation of Judah. God is therefore described as a divorcee by both Jeremiah and Isaiah (Jeremiah 3:8; Isaiah 50:1).

Malachi recorded that God hates divorce. This doesn't mean that God hates *divorced people*, rather that he hates the treachery and breaking of vows that lead to divorce (Malachi 2:14–16). In fact, no one knows the pain of divorce more than God himself, who suffered his wife Israel's infidelity for hundreds of years.

When Jesus taught about divorce, he reminded his hearers

about God's relationship with Israel by using the word "hard-hearted". This word was invented by the Greek translators of the Old Testament and wasn't used in everyday Greek, so anyone who did use it was quoting an Old Testament text. It is only used twice in the Old Testament (Deuteronomy 10:16; Jeremiah 4:4), and the second instance is in a passage about God's divorce from Israel (Jeremiah 3–4). In choosing to use this particular word, Jesus was therefore deliberately reminding his listeners that God didn't "divorce" Israel until the point when she was sinning "hard-heartedly" – that is, stubbornly and continually. His conclusion, then, is clear – husbands and wives, too, should work hard at being reconciled before considering the option of divorce.

In making this point, Jesus had actually digressed from the main topic of discussion. His questioners had asked him about divorce but he had wanted to talk about marriage, and especially the ideal of lifelong commitment. God made Adam and Eve in perfection, to live together for ever, but sin came along and Jesus recognized this by saying that God introduced divorce because of "your hard-heartedness". He wasn't saying that only ancient Jews were sinful – "you" refers to everyone, in every time and place: human nature is still the same, thousands of years later, among followers of all religions and none, Christians as well as Jews. Jesus explained that because of our sin, God *allows* divorce. But that doesn't mean divorce *should* happen. It is always the result of one partner's or both partners' sin in breaking their marriage vows.

The scandal was that many men wanted it to be easier to divorce. A man could divorce his wife if she broke her marriage vows, but often he wanted a divorce when there were no valid reasons for it – even simply because he was fed up with her. However, as long as his wife kept her vows, he did not have grounds to divorce her. The Jews resolved this "problem" by inventing the new form of easy divorce. We would probably have called it a no-fault divorce, but the term they used was "Any Cause" because of the Bible text they based it on.

They derived this new type of divorce from Scripture using an ingenious legal manoeuvre. In Moses' legislation about divorce, the literal phrase "a cause of nakedness" (Deuteronomy 24:1) had always been taken to mean "adultery", but they argued that the word "nakedness" by itself implies adultery, so the word "cause" must have *extra* meaning. Moses, they claimed, must therefore have been referring to two grounds for divorce: "a cause" *and* "nakedness". They concluded that "nakedness" meant "Adultery" but "a cause" meant "Any Cause", and that way they created the new law of divorce for "Any Cause".

By the time of Jesus most Jews had adopted this new law, including the two most prolific Jewish authors of the day, Philo and Josephus. In fact, they both talked about divorce for "Any Cause" without reference to any other grounds for divorce that existed.[2] Both men and women approved of this new law. Men liked it because they could get divorced for anything without needing to go through a humiliating trial and women liked it because they got their 200 *zuz*. It became the "righteous" way to divorce, and Matthew even commended Joseph for planning to use this type of "quiet" divorce, rather than divorcing Mary publicly in court for her apparent unfaithfulness (Matthew 1:19).

But although most Jews used and accepted the new "Any Cause" divorce, it was still a topic of heated debate. One group of rabbis in particular, the Shammaites, stood vehemently against it. They said that Moses' words "a cause of nakedness" in Deuteronomy 24:1 were a single phrase so it didn't refer to two types of divorce – it referred to no divorce "except for sexual immorality" (i.e. adultery). They had an ongoing argument about this with another group of rabbis, the Hillelites, who wanted to replace the Old Testament grounds for divorce with the new "Any Cause" divorce. This was the context for their coming to Jesus and asking him, "Is it lawful to divorce one's wife for any cause?" (Matthew 19:3). Jesus answered by agreeing with the Shammaites – that is, defending the traditional interpretation of the text – and he even quoted their slogan that Deuteronomy 24:1 referred to no divorce "except for sexual immorality" (Matthew 19:9).

Most modern readers will get a completely different impression when they read the question: "Is it lawful to divorce one's wife for any cause?" Unless you know that everyone was debating the "Any Cause" divorce, you wouldn't think they were asking him about this; it just looks as if they are asking Jesus if he approves of divorce in general. A similar confusion might have happened even if the Jews had called it a no-fault divorce and they'd asked Jesus: "Is it lawful to divorce one's wife for no fault?" Try pretending you have never heard of a no-fault divorce and read this as plain language. It sounds like they are asking Jesus if one can divorce a wife for being faultless or, perhaps, for acting as though she was right all the time. If you don't know the jargon, the plain language can be very confusing!

In Jesus' day everyone knew the legal jargon because everyone was talking about the new "Any Cause" divorce. It was such a hot topic that Mark didn't even bother to include the term "Any Cause". He records the question as: "Is it lawful for a man to divorce his wife?" (Mark 10:2). It was actually a nonsense question, because the Pharisees didn't ask Jesus if *he* allowed it – they asked if *the law* allowed it – and everyone knew that it did. It is rather like asking: "Should a sixteen-year-old be allowed to drink?" It's a nonsense question because, of course, they'd die if they did not drink. Today we automatically make sense of the question by mentally adding the word "alcohol". In the same way, Jews in Jesus' day would automatically add the words "for any cause" after the question, "Is it lawful to divorce your wife?" It was the obvious subject of any question about divorce at the time.

However, once the debate was over and the "Any Cause" divorce had become the only type of divorce available, the technical term "Any Cause" was forgotten very quickly. It's rather like the English concept of "divorce by co-respondent" that was frequently cited along with lurid details in the popular newspapers of my youth. Nowadays most people have forgotten what it means, and it sounds as if you can be divorced for having a penpal! Actually a "co-respondent" is someone you commit adultery with – look it up in a good dictionary. This once commonly known legal term is now as unremembered as "Any Cause".

Jesus did succeed in ending easy divorces among Christians, though not among Jews. He reasserted the principle that marriages should be lifelong and should only end after marriage vows have been repeatedly broken – and no believer should do this! In reality, of course, it does happen. We are all too capable of sin, and sometimes a believer has to enact a divorce, just as God eventually had to divorce Israel.

Unfortunately Christians threw out divorce on the grounds of neglect along with the "Any Cause" divorce. The church misunderstood Jesus' teaching and made divorce so difficult that only the very rich and influential could obtain one. So although the church stopped the powerless being divorced against their will, many powerless people were locked into abusive marriages. The chapter "Marital Abuse" shows how Jesus' original audience would have understood his teaching on this, and how this tragedy could have been avoided.

Notes

1. Mishnah Gittin 9.10.
2. Philo, *Special Laws* 3.30; Josephus, *Antiquities* 4.253.

Marital Abuse

I couldn't figure out why Nick (not his real name) had given up his well-paid day job and flown across several time zones to help me publicize a rather scholarly book on biblical divorce. Over coffee one day he told me about an old school friend who joined the same church as him after she'd got married. Occasional bruises and unexpected absences soon indicated that her marriage was going badly wrong. Nick wasn't surprised when she left her husband, but the minister and elders of the church were shocked. They sympathized, yet said that as a Christian she had to trust God and return to her husband. She protested that they had no idea how bad his temper was, but in the end she did return to him. One day, no one knows why, her husband went after her with a gun. As she ran from the house, he shot her dead. Nick decided from that day to do all he could to look for biblical solutions to such problems.

Scandals of abuse existed in New Testament times, but Old Testament law allowed women to divorce their husbands long before the abuse got too bad. Examples that we have recorded in Jewish law codes of the first two centuries include the case of a woman who was ordered by her husband never to visit her parents and another where the wife was forced to pour all the household waste water onto the manure heap instead of using the normal drain (think of the smelly splatter!).[1] The courts agreed that these were cases of abuse, and the women had the right to a divorce. Of course they heard many thousands of other cases, but these two were recorded as a benchmark so that in cases of the same or worse abuse, other judges would know that the victims had the right to a divorce.

The Jewish leaders learned this approach from the Bible, which establishes a general law by specifying the minimum requirements. Exodus 21 details the law of marital neglect by listing the minimum support that must be given to a wife: food, clothing and love (Exodus 21:10–11). The law said that these were the minimum requirements even to wives who had been slaves, so it is clear that they were also due to free-born wives and to husbands. These three were the basis of Jewish marriage vows: the husband had to provide food and cloth, while the wife had to make meals and clothing, and both had to give themselves in love to each other.

Lawyers can sometimes seem to ruin everything, especially romance. The rabbinic lawyers shortly before Jesus' day decided to define exactly how little should be regarded as neglect: they stated how much food and clothing the husband had to provide, how many meals his wife had to make, and even how often they had to make love. A man who worked normal hours had to do his "duty" once a week, but a travelling salesman was allowed a month off and a sailor was allowed six months off. An unemployed man, however, was expected to perform every night![2]

If either partner neglected to provide food, clothing or love, the other could take them to court and get a divorce. Cases of adultery or physical neglect (failure to provide food or clothing) were straightforward, and divorce was granted if the wronged partner wanted it. But in cases of emotional neglect (i.e. refusal of physical love) the rabbis created time for reconciliation by imposing a long series of fines on the reluctant partner. A husband was fined by having to add to his wife's dowry (which she took with her if they were divorced), and a wife was fined by reducing this dowry. This continued until the money ran out or they made up.

The important question for Christians is how Jesus and Paul interpreted this Old Testament law of divorce for neglect and abuse. One problem the church has grappled with for centuries is that Jesus appeared to forbid divorce "for any cause… except sexual immorality" (Matthew 19:3–9, ESV). The common interpretation until recently has been that Jesus allowed divorce only for adultery. This has been very difficult to understand pastorally and seems absurdly contradictory of other biblical principles, since it appears to condone abuse and abandonment. Even as early as AD 200 the Church Father Origen was puzzled by it. He said that if a wife was trying to poison her husband, or if she deliberately killed their baby, then for her husband "to endure sins of such heinousness which seem to be worse than adultery or fornication, will appear to be irrational."[3] Nevertheless, Jesus' teaching appeared plain, so the church followed it.

This mystery has been recently solved by research in ancient Jewish documents where we find that the phrase "Any Cause" divorce was a legal term equivalent to the modern no-fault divorce (see the chapter "No-fault Divorce"). By means of a legalistic interpretation of the phrase "cause of immorality" in Deuteronomy 24:1, some rabbis allowed divorce for both "Immorality" and "Any Cause". When they asked Jesus what he thought, he confirmed that this phrase referred merely to divorce for adultery (nothing about "except sexual immorality"). He totally rejected the newly invented divorce for "Any Cause". The misunderstanding through the centuries has been the belief that Jesus was referring to *all* grounds for divorce rather than the "Any Cause" divorce specifically.

Jesus actually said nothing about the law of divorce for neglect and abuse in Exodus 21. This was partly because he wasn't asked about it and partly because it wasn't a topic of debate like the text in Deuteronomy 24. All rabbis still accepted these biblical grounds of neglect of food, clothing and love, and ancient Jewish marriage contracts found in caves near the Dead Sea show that these three requirements were incorporated into Jewish marriage vows. Every couple would promise each other to provide "food, clothing and bed" (a euphemism for sexual intercourse), just as it says in Exodus 21.

Jesus' silence on the subject isn't unusual – there were many other things about which he said nothing, including the biggest issues in this area of ethics: he said nothing at all about rape, incest, or sex before marriage (an omission which every youth leader regrets!). But the reason he didn't speak about these matters is because he agreed with the clear teaching about them in the Old Testament, and since all Jews accepted this too, it was not an issue.

Jesus certainly wasn't silent when he *disagreed* about something! For example, when he was asked about divorce he took the opportunity to point out other areas where he opposed the current teaching on marriage. He disagreed with those Pharisees who thought that divorce was "commanded" after adultery (Matthew 19:7–8); he rejected polygamy, which was still allowed by most Palestinian Jews (Matthew 19:5; see the chapter "Polygamy"); and he denied that marriage was compulsory, as taught by most Jews (Matthew 19:12; see the chapter "Ineligible Bachelor"). None of these subjects were ones Jesus had been asked about; he deliberately brought them up himself because he wanted to tell the Jews everything they were getting wrong in the area of marriage and divorce law. As with the other ethical areas he was silent about, Jesus did not say anything about cases of neglect or abuse because there was no need to. The Old Testament law was totally accepted by everyone and there was therefore no reason for him to specifically affirm it – he would only have needed to speak about it if he disagreed with it.

Arguments from silence are not always very safe and we are fortunate that Paul gives some very positive affirmation of this teaching. Paul, unlike Jesus, had to speak about the three marital obligations in Exodus 21:11 because his Gentile converts needed to learn the biblical principles that were well known to Jews. In 1 Corinthians 7 he pointed out that a husband and wife's marriage obligations included "love" for each other, not to deprive each other, and to provide each other with "worldly things" (i.e. food and clothing: vv. 3–5, 33–34). These three obligations also turn up in Ephesians where the church is portrayed as a bride of Christ who "loves... nourishes and cherishes" her – or, more literally, "loves... feeds and keeps her warm" (Ephesians 5:28–29).

Paul was responding to members of the Corinthian church who wanted to leave their non-Christian partners. One woman had already "separated from" her husband, which in Roman law meant she had already divorced him. Roman law required no paperwork or court appearance; as soon as you separated with the intention to divorce, your marriage was legally over and you were available for remarriage. Paul said that non-Christian marriages were valid in God's eyes (1 Corinthians 7:12–14) and he couldn't allow divorce when there were no valid grounds. This woman shouldn't have left her husband, so Paul told her to attempt reconciliation and to remain unmarried because a new marriage would make reconciliation much more difficult (1 Corinthians 7:10–11)!

As a believer, this woman presumably obeyed Paul and the marriage was re-established. But what about the opposite situation when a non-believer divorced a believer? Paul deals with this in verse 15, saying that such believers are "no longer bound" or, literally, "no longer enslaved". No – this doesn't mean that Paul regarded marriage as slavery! The concept comes from the wording of Jewish divorce certificates which said: "You are now free to marry anyone you wish" (as Jewish lawyers pointed out, they used the exact wording found on freedom-from-slavery certificates). Paul wasn't commenting here on whether they could get divorced because that had already happened – as we have said, in Roman law the marriage was already over – but he was telling them, having been divorced, that they were free to remarry. This fits in with the Old Testament law of neglect, because someone divorced against their will has, in effect, been abandoned, and therefore their divorce is based on biblical grounds.

The principle followed by Paul and the Old Testament law is that only the wronged partner has the right to initiate divorce. In Moses' law, the person who was neglected could demand freedom from the marriage. But what if the other person initiates divorce? The Corinthian woman who divorced her husband without any proper grounds was told to go back and ask for reconciliation because she had no right to end the marriage. This meant that the choice now lay with the husband she had abandoned to either accept her back or accept the divorce. Any man or woman who was divorced against their will without biblical grounds had the right to end the marriage because they were the wronged partner and were "no longer bound" (1 Corinthians 7:15).

In all these details, Paul agreed with Jesus that no-fault divorces were wrong. Jesus rejected the "Any Cause" divorces of Jewish society and Paul rejected the "divorce by separation" of Roman society. Jesus demanded that there should be valid grounds for ending the marriage, such as adultery, and Paul affirmed that these valid grounds included neglect and abandonment.

My friend Nick realized that this rediscovery of ancient legal terminology wasn't just obscure scholarly research – it meant that the New Testament allowed divorce for abandonment and abuse.

He now saw that Jesus' teaching "made sense" again; faithful believers could be set free from marriages in which they were trapped as victims of abuse or neglect. For him, spreading this news is a mission to prevent others suffering like his murdered friend. The church has a vital role in encouraging and supporting healthy marriages, but we also have a clear responsibility to seek biblical remedies for those who are suffering in abusive marriages.

Notes

1. Mishnah Ketuvot 7.4–5.
2. Mishnah Ketuvot 5.5–8.
3. *Commentary on Matthew* II.14.24.

Unfair Loans

King Croesus of Lydia became the richest man in the world by being honest. He is often credited with inventing coins, but his father and predecessor, King Alyattes, first made gold coins in about 600 BC. King Alyattes claimed his coins were made of electrum (a natural form of gold that contains some silver), but he devalued them by adding extra silver so they were only 60 per cent gold, and disguised this by adding gold-coloured copper. The merchants soon caught on and rejected them. Croesus, however, produced the world's first pure gold coins by melting all the silver out of electrum – a technically difficult process. They made him extremely rich because everyone trusted them and bought them from him to trade with.

Coinage and paper currency is so normal for us that we can't imagine what it was like when every sale involved time-consuming barter, especially because the goods being exchanged could be of uncertain value. Coins have a fixed weight and value and are authenticated so that both seller and buyer can trust them. They are also much easier to carry than barter goods such as sheep or pots of grain. The Chinese also introduced money at about the same time, though their coins were in the shapes of small spades and daggers – perhaps indicating the two main sources of wealth: farming and fighting.

The invention of money created a new way of getting rich – making money from money itself. You could exchange currency, buy and sell commodities without ever handing over any goods, or simply lend money. Each of these involved a percentage for the dealer which could range from fair to crippling.

At the time of Jesus, coinage was still considered "new technology" and people were naturally suspicious of it. The Jews invented a new word for coin-based wealth – *mammon* – a word which encapsulated everything bad about money. Jesus summed up popular feeling when he said: "You cannot serve God and Mammon" (Matthew 6:24; Luke 16:13) – that is, beware lest coins become your god. But although coins might have been mistrusted, they had become a necessary part of Jewish life. In villages goods could still be exchanged via barter and promises, but coins were needed for wages, buying food in the market, giving a dowry for your bride and paying taxes.

Many of Jesus' parables were about the modern realities of money. He told stories about discovering a buried money hoard, using money to set up a business, looking for lost dowry coins, and even a parable about "creative accounting". This particular parable was about an "unrighteous steward" (Luke 16:1–9) – an accounts manager who gets fired. Before leaving, the steward calls in several customers who owe money and makes a deal with them – he reduces the size of the amount they owe. He does this in the hope that they'll return the favours later. We can't be sure whether he was stretching a discretionary discount for prompt payment or whether he was simply being fraudulent. The story implies that he was acting dishonestly and that the boss found out, but then comes the twist in the story. Seeing how cleverly he'd acted, his boss praised him and presumably decided to keep him on!

We might conclude that Jesus approved of the steward's dishonesty, but the moral that he drew from the parable was this: If the unjust can plan ahead, then we too should plan for eternity.

Then, as now, money attracted fraud and scandal, and

this was especially true when it came to taxes. Tax collectors added a mark up or simply cheated the people, intimidating and extorting them with the help of their bodyguards. John the Baptist spoke out against this (Luke 3:14) and when the tax-collector Zacchaeus repented, he returned all the money that he had overcharged people (Luke 19:1–9).

Another financial scandal in Jesus' day was surprisingly caused by Old Testament law. This was because the poor were kept impoverished by a law which discouraged loans. Two aspects of Moses' law were responsible for this. First, a lender wasn't allowed to charge fellow Jews any interest (Deuteronomy 23:20). This law made sense in an isolated desert community, but in Jesus' day inflation meant that a lender would not only fail to make any money, but would actually lose money if he offered it at zero interest. The result was that a Jew who wanted to start a business or borrow for a daughter's dowry, for example, would be unable to get a loan.

The second problem when making loans was the law of Sabbath Year – the cancellation of all loans every seven years (Deuteronomy 15:1–3). This sounds like a good policy for the poor – and it was in Moses' time – but in the first century it wasn't working any more. The law was made for agricultural times, with the aim of ensuring that every family was able to keep their small plot of land for subsistence farming. If they got into financial difficulty, they could sell the land's leasehold but not the freehold, because every fifty years all land reverted to the family who owned it originally. Israel had neglected to keep this law for most of its history, but it was reintroduced shortly before Jesus' day when there was a new enthusiasm to obey God's law. However, since most land was now owned by foreigners or rich families, the law had become unworkable. The shameful part of this was that it didn't improve things for the poor; it simply meant that lenders were reluctant to make any long-term loans.

A poor person now had to find a lender who was prepared both to lend money without getting any interest *and* to lose it all if he wasn't repaid soon enough. No one was willing to lend on these terms until Rabbi Hillel came up with a nice legal loophole that allowed lenders to protect themselves.[1] His new rule was that lenders could give loans to the Temple and for the Temple to then lend this money to the customer. The lender would be quite sure that his money was safe because the Temple wasn't subject to the Sabbath Year law of cancelling loans. This imaginative solution put a stop to this particular financial scandal by helping the poor tremendously.

Unfortunately, the church did not learn from this, as it continued to prohibit charging interest on personal and business loans, making it impossible for those who needed to borrow money to do so. It was not until the sixteenth century that a prominent European banking family, the Fuggers, employed a scholar called Eck to investigate the morality of lending at interest. In 1515 he concluded that businesses would be helped if 5 per cent interest was allowed, though loans to the poor should still be interest-free. This revolution helped business no end, and to start with helped the poor too. But soon interest was also charged on loans to the poor, at higher and higher rates. Today it is the poor who pay the highest interest on loans. Those who get short-term loans against their next salary (so-called "payday loans") can pay an APR of over 1000 per cent.

Jesus was not against the use of money, even when people used it to make more wealth. In his parable of the talents each servant was given a large weight of gold by his master – a talent weighs about the same as a sack of cement, which is a lot of gold! When the master returned, the servants were judged by how much profit they'd made. The one who had buried his gold to keep it safe was reprimanded and told that he should have banked the gold and earned interest on it at the very least; the others, who had made a profit, were commended. Of course, we can't be sure that Jesus approved of investing money or lending with interest merely because he told parables about it. However, in this parable the master is clearly supposed to be Jesus himself, so he does seem to give at least tacit approval to such practices.

Does God give financial rewards? The Jews of Jesus' day thought so; they believed that if you lived a righteous life your good deeds were stored in heaven as treasure (i.e. capital) and that God paid you interest by giving you good things on earth.[2] Jesus' listeners thought he was going to agree with this teaching when he urged them to "Store up treasure in heaven" (Matthew 6:19–20). You can almost hear the crowds joining in to complete the saying: "… and you will get interest on earth." But Jesus *didn't* go on to say this. Leaving out a promise of earthly financial rewards was a shock to his listeners and it is one of the most significant silences in Jesus' teaching.

The ubiquity and usefulness of money makes the Jewish suspicion of Mammon seem antiquated and unrealistic. In many ways, Jesus was ahead of his time when he spoke in favour of making profits from capital and even in his recognition of the complexities and sometimes hazy "morality" of the world of money.

However, when it came to personal profit, Jesus issued two severe warnings. First, don't expect God to play at being investment banker by giving interest on good deeds – if they are done for the sake of buying an easy life, then they aren't "good". The prosperity gospel did not start with Jesus! And second, watch out that money does not become your goal in life, because that goal can become your god.

Notes

1. The *Prosbul*, meaning "through the court" – see Mishnah Shebi'it 10.3. The need for this rule shows that this aspect of Sabbath Years was being practised as normal law in Israel during Jesus' day.
2. Mishnah Peah 1.1.

Oaths and Curses

More ancient Roman curses have been found in Britain than in the rest of the Roman Empire added together. They have survived the damp climate as they were scratched on small sheets of lead (about 6 cm across) which were rolled up and stuffed into the crevices of walls or dropped into drains or graves. Most of them were found in the beautiful city of Bath, especially in and around the ancient Roman baths themselves. The vast majority of these curses are directed at thieves, probably because bath-houses were ideal places to steal clothes and bags that were stored while their owners bathed. These curses called upon the gods to attack the body and mind of the thief in extraordinarily vicious ways. Usually the curser didn't bother to ask for the stolen goods to be returned – what they wanted most was revenge.

The curses found outside Britain are fewer but more varied. They include curses on love rivals and rival charioteers – for example: "Bind the legs and hands and head and heart of Victoricus the charioteer of the Blue team…" and "May they be broken, may they be dragged (on the ground), may they be destroyed." Often the curse was seen by no one except the person writing it, who then rolled it up and hid it, so the Romans didn't expect them to work by auto-suggestion – they depended on the gods to enact the curse.

The New Testament frequently criticizes cursing (Luke 6:28; Romans 3:14; 12:14; James 3:9–10; 1 Peter 3:9), although Jewish curses were actually very mild compared with Roman ones. And because the Jews probably realized that God was likely to ignore requests that cursed people, they devised a subtler method of invoking misfortune upon someone. They created the *Korban* oath, which was a kind of self-cursing – it asked God to punish them if they ever helped the particular person they hated. This meant that they could piously deny their enemy any help when they needed it, even if they were a close neighbour or, scandalously, even a close relative. Jesus utterly condemned this practice (Mark 7:9–13).

We can feel smug in the knowledge that we don't do this kind of thing any more. Very few people in modern societies make genuine curses – not because we wish only good to our neighbours, but because we don't believe curses work. Of course "swearing" is prolific, but this isn't the same as a real curse – though it doesn't mean that using modern swear words is harmless.

It's surprising how many of our expletives come from old curse formulae, especially the ones that date back a long way and are now considered acceptable. For example, ancient Roman curses were often addressed to Hecate, the goddess of witchcraft, and many people still say "By Heck!" Similarly, we say things like "By God!", "God!", "Damn you!" (i.e. "God damn you!"), "Cor blimey!" (i.e. "God blind me if…!"), "By George!" (i.e. "By God!"), "OMG!" (i.e. "Oh, my God!"), "Bloody" (i.e. "By our Lady!"), or simply "Jesus Christ!" A schoolteacher in a deprived area told me that he had once shocked his class by mentioning Jesus, because they'd never heard the name "Jesus" used as anything but a swear word.

Jesus, as we'd expect, had very high standards for his followers and he stood against all uses of oath language. Some Jews used swear words to emphasize that they were telling the truth, but Jesus told them not to swear at all – to simply let "Yes" mean "Yes!" and "No" mean "No!" (Matthew 5:33–37). Some modern believers refuse to take oaths in court because of this teaching, so

British courts let them make an "affirmation" instead of an oath. But Jesus was speaking about a much bigger issue than official oaths – he was criticizing the everyday use of swear words for emphasis. He said his followers should be known as people who simply and consistently tell the truth, without needing an oath to convey that they really mean it.

Jesus also spoke against using swear words to express anger and hatred or even contempt. When expounding the commandment "You shall not murder", he applied it even to the use of "*raca*" – an Aramaic term of contempt meaning something like "idiot" or "oaf" (Matthew 5:22). A couple of generations' later, Rabbi Eleazar ben Simeon brought shame on himself by realizing he had failed to apply this teaching. He was travelling home when he came across an ugly man who greeted him: "Peace be upon you, Sir." Without thinking, the rabbi answered: "You oaf [*raca*]! Is everyone in your town so ugly?" The man replied: "I do not know, Sir, but please complain about my ugliness to the craftsman who made me." Horrified by the realization that he'd criticized God, the rabbi begged the man's forgiveness and walked respectfully behind him, like a servant, for the rest of his journey home. It turned out that the man came from the rabbi's own town, so all his disciples witnessed his shame.[1]

Paul warned against using speech to hurt or offend others (e.g. Colossians 3:8; Ephesians 4:29) and advised Titus to stick to "sound speech which cannot be condemned, so that your opponents will have nothing bad to say about you" (Titus 2:8). Paul also said that the language we use should be "salty" (Colossians 4:6) – that is, seasoned with good things (N.B. *not* its opposite connotation in English, which suggests the unrestrained language of sailors!). He advised, too, against coarse jokes and obscenities expressed in a light-hearted way (Ephesians 5:4).

Jesus even condemned using the kinds of euphemisms that

avoid real swear words. Jews learned from the Old Testament that making a vow (even a casual vow) was extremely serious. If they jokingly said: "By God, I'll give a hundred shekels to anyone who can find my door-key", then they had to be prepared to pay up. The same went for vows that were made rashly, though a rash vow made by a woman could be annulled by her father or husband (Numbers 30:2–15). This is probably because it was her father or husband who would be liable to pay the cost, so he needed the power to annul any vow she might maliciously make to impoverish him. The Jews invented a way to avoid making binding vows by using euphemisms instead of genuine vow formulae, such as "By the Temple" instead of "By God". Jesus called this hypocrisy and said that these euphemisms were as wrong as the real thing (Matthew 23:16–22).

The way people speak can mark them out geographically and socially and it should also mark out those who are serious about respecting God and fellow humans. Obscene language is as disrespectful to people as pornography; crude language can flame anger into hatred; naming God or pagan gods merely to make speech more "colourful" dishonours our creator (see more on blasphemy in the chapter "Unforgivable Blasphemy"); and substituting euphemisms merely confirms that language spoken in this way is wrong.

Jesus regarded shameful language as more defiling than faeces – he said that what comes out of our mouths can make us more impure than food which goes into them and comes out the other end (Matthew 15:17–18). He also reminded us that we will have to account for every word we have spoken (Matthew 12:36). Paul presented a helpful picture of how this judgment will happen: a fire will burn up all those words and actions in our lives that are not worthy of our new life with God. In this way, only what is pure enough will enter heaven (1 Corinthians

3:12–15). On that basis I suspect that my collected words to date may form a very thin volume.

Notes

1. Babylonian Talmud Taanit 20b.

Bitterness and Hatred

A rotten potato smells far worse than a rotten apple. As a teenager I used to deliver potatoes to hotels and restaurants for a Saturday job. I'd haul the sacks on to my shoulder and tread carefully down steep stairs and narrow corridors where there was no room for any lifting machinery. Now and then I'd heave up a sack and it would burst in a shower of foul-smelling black slush. A rotten potato at the bottom had turned all its neighbours into a stinking mush that weakened the thick paper sack. The smell would stay on me all day until I could go home for a bath.

In its ability to harbour bad things, unforgiveness is even worse. A small offence by someone can settle in your mind, infecting your thoughts and memories until everything connected with that person makes you unreasonably angry. The next time they do the slightest thing wrong, you explode like an unopened can of beans on a bonfire.

The Jews at Qumran near the Dead Sea had to learn how to resolve conflicts because they lived together, like a huge family. Long-lasting grudges could turn the peace of their isolated community into a silence filled with stifled anger that would lead to frustrated outbursts of temper. To try to prevent this, the community adapted a rule from the Old Testament law of love (Leviticus 19:17–18). They said that if someone wronged you, you should rebuke them before the sun went down, so that they could make recompense or apologize. You should speak the truth in order to help that person avoid further sin. If they didn't accept their fault, then you should invite friends to help both of you sort things out. And if you still couldn't resolve your differences, you should take the matter to the whole community that same day. They certainly took conflict seriously!

They had an additional rule which they adhered to very strictly: if you chose *not* to rebuke someone on the day that an offence occurred, you must then never mention that incident in the future. You'll know as well as I do that when we have an argument with someone and lose our temper, we're tempted to drag up all the unresolved conflicts we've had with them in the past and get angry about them all over again. The Qumran community prevented this by punishing anyone who brought up previous conflicts in anger – they excluded that person from their community meals for a period.[1]

This method of conflict resolution was taken up by Christians. Jesus commended the three-stage process of confrontation: one-to-one; then before witnesses; and finally before the whole congregation (Matthew 18:15–17). He also told a parable to emphasize the need for speedy reconciliation (Matthew 5:25–26). And Paul encouraged believers to "Speak the truth in love" and told them to do it without delay: "The sun must not set on your anger" (Ephesians 4:15, 26).

This teaching at Qumran may help us understand Jesus' difficult saying about anger being similar to murder (Matthew 5:21–22). Jesus himself displayed anger when appropriate (e.g. Mark 3:5; John 2:15–17), but in that passage he said that even calling someone a "*raca*" (Aramaic for "idiot" or "oaf") was an act deserving of punishment in hell. Since he said this shortly before his parable about settling disputes quickly (Matthew 5:25–26), it is likely that the "anger" Jesus was talking about here was the anger of unresolved conflicts – the type of anger that Qumran Jews punished when people brought up old conflicts to exacerbate a new argument. This regurgitation of unforgiven offences can fuel a single inflammatory remark into a sustained angry exchange that results in long-term hatred.

To refuse to forgive someone who repented was a scandal in Judaism that was considered worse than the original offence. On the Day of Atonement (when Jews repent of all their sins of the past year), any unforgiveness on your part was believed to "block" your own forgiveness. They believed that if you had a grudge against someone and refused to forgive them after they had repented, then God would not forgive you.[2] Jesus agreed with this and taught it four times: in his parable of the unforgiving servant, in the Lord's Prayer, in other teaching about prayer, and in the passage about anger, where he says you should be reconciled with those with whom you have a grudge before bringing God your worship or offering (Matthew 18:23–35; Luke 11:4; Mark 5:25; Matthew 5:23–24).

Jesus' disciples were understandably wary about this emphasis. They asked how many times they had to forgive a repentant person. Jesus said seventy times seven – that is, 490 separate occasions (Matthew 18:21–22)! We could regard this as simply a very large number, but Jesus said this because it was the number of years that God had forgiven Israel before they were sent into exile. The seventy-year exile was calculated from the number of Sabbath rests that Israel had not given the land (2 Chronicles 36:21). Every seventh year they were supposed to leave farmland uncultivated, so that it didn't get worked out by intensive farming. During the Exile, God gave the land all the rest it had missed. Of course, the purpose was not to give the land a backdated holiday, but to punish Israel for having rejected God's good law for all those Sabbath years. When Israel returned from exile the people repented and re-instituted the seven-year farming cycle. Because God forgave Israel for these 490 years of disobedience, Jesus said we should follow God's example in the number of times we forgive people – not literally 490 times, but for as many times as someone needs our forgiveness.

We should also rebuke someone who sins when the offence is not against us personally because they need to be reminded that it is wrong. This must be done in love – the command "Love your neighbour" comes straight after the command to rebuke (Leviticus 19:17–18). It is so easy to condemn others and if you can't imagine yourself falling into the same sin, then it is probably better to find someone else to "rebuke" them – perhaps someone less holy than you! Later rabbis said, on the basis of this verse, that a master can be rebuked even by his disciple.[3] Unless we can understand the temptations of others, and long for them to repent and be forgiven, we will not be able to rebuke in love.

Forgiveness can be seen as letting people off too easily. But forgiveness depends on genuine repentance (Luke 17:3) and being forgiven doesn't necessarily remove all practical consequences. God forgave David for plotting Uriah's death in order to take his wife, but despite David's repentance, Uriah stayed dead (2 Samuel 11; Psalm 51). Offences involving violence and theft are likely to result in sanctions or safeguards even if they are repented.

Should we accept repentance if we don't think it is genuine? Ultimately that isn't our problem. Forgiveness on our part is a matter of our attitude and our contribution to reconciliation; it is not a matter of justice. We can trust God to recognize a person's sincerity and to judge justly. We are merely called to accept the repentance that is offered and leave the final judgment to God. And if we do not forgive we give safe haven to a malignant bitterness that will eventually consume us. Jesus was in complete agreement with the Jews on this particular matter: both were adamant that unforgiveness can be a greater scandal than the sin that needed to be forgiven.

Notes

1. See *Rule of the Community* 5.24 – 6.1; *Damascus Document* 9:16–24.
2. Mishnah Yoma 8.9. For the "Unforgivable Sin", see the chapter "Unforgivable Blasphemy".
3. Babylonian Talmud Baba Metzi'a 31a.

Good and Bad Luck

Florence Nightingale's superiors were aghast when she ordered medical supplies for the Crimean War in advance by predicting the number of men who would become injured or diseased. They held the belief that because humans act with free will and, on top of that, God does what he wants, it was simply not possible for the future to be predicted. How could anyone forecast the percentage of men who would be injured in a cavalry charge, or the proportion that would get malaria? Nevertheless, Florence's predictions were proved correct and, because of them, fewer men died. The importance of the study of medical statistics was recognized from that point on.

Throughout history people have always believed that things did not depend on mere chance. Ancient Greeks believed in the Fates, who had control of each person's destiny, spinning the threads of their life and deciding its length. Ancient Romans worshipped the goddess Fortuna, though she wasn't always helpful – she spun a wheel at random to determine good or bad circumstances for you. This "Lady Luck" remained popular even among Christians who transformed the blessing "Good luck" into "God speed" ("spede" was Middle English for "luck"). From the time of Augustine in the fifth century, the church tried to suppress such phrases as scandalous superstition, but failed. In the evangelist John Wesley's journal for 1763 he records a group of ministers wishing him "Good luck in the name of the Lord", and few Christians today regard saying "Good luck" as scandalously pagan.

The Old Testament writers believed that God was in charge of everything. Even throwing a lot (which was like flipping a coin) did not give a random result because God was in overall control (Proverbs 16:33). However, contradictorily, they also recognized that things did appear to happen by chance at times. When an arrow killed King Jehoshaphat, it looked like random bad luck. He was disguised as a normal soldier, so no one aimed at him in particular, and the arrow just happened to hit a vulnerable slit in his armour at the right angle to penetrate it. The original text says of the archer who killed him: "he drew his bow innocently" – which is as near as Hebrew can get to expressing the idea of an unplanned random event (1 Kings 22:34). And yet, the reason Jehoshaphat was disguised was because a prophet had predicted that he would be killed in the battle – so even this apparently random event was controlled by God.

Does this mean that God decides where every raindrop falls and where every germ infects? Some theologians (called "deists") regard the world as completely mechanistic – that is, God set everything going and now simply lets things happen according to the laws of science. Others (called "theists") believe God may occasionally interrupt with a miracle. At the end of this spectrum are Christian thinkers who say that God directs and decides every single event, down to the atomic level.

If God directs absolutely everything, it is difficult to find room for human freedom and it seems pointless to pray because God has already decided what to do and what to make us want to pray for. And God has determined exactly what we are thinking right now! (It all gets very confusing.) For such reasons, most Christian thinkers hold a view somewhere in the middle of these extremes – that is, they are moderate theists. They believe that God works in the world alongside the laws of nature, while allowing limited human freedom; that he occasionally interrupts normality by doing something which we regard as a miracle; and that he often works in the background in ways we usually don't notice.

Jesus, too, appears to have been a moderate theist. This is, of course, a strange way to talk about Jesus, partly because the distinction between deists and theists didn't start till the sixteenth century and partly because we can't pigeonhole Jesus! Nevertheless, in the Gospels Jesus assumed that God was involved in every detail, while at the same time he implied that prayer and human freedom are realities. He encouraged his followers to pray not only for big things ("faith can move mountains") but also little things like daily food, and he assumed that God was in charge of everything – even what people did (John 19:11: "You could do nothing… unless it is given to you from above"). On the other hand, Jesus said that God knows how many hairs we have and knows when each sparrow dies (Luke 12:6–7; Matthew 10:29–31), though he didn't say that God actively kills sparrows or hair follicles.

Jesus thought differently from most Jews of his day about this. They believed that everything was specifically purposed by God, but Jesus denied this – at least, he denied that we could *know* the purpose of most events. For example, when he was asked about the people who were killed when a tower collapsed in Siloam, Jesus' answer was the opposite of what most people would have thought: he said that those who were killed were no worse sinners than others (Luke 13:4–5). On another occasion, when he was asked whether a man was blind because of his own sin or his parents' sin, Jesus said that it was due to neither, though his illness would bring glory to God; then, to prove it, Jesus healed him (John 9:2–7). In other words, the bad things that had happened were not part of a plan by God for reward or retribution.

Old Testament prophets implied that God picks and chooses who to send rain on (Jeremiah 14:22; Amos 4:7). However, this doesn't mean that he *always* does this. Sometimes God creates a drought to show his displeasure, or ends a drought to help those who trust him, but normally rain falls indiscriminately. We know this because observation tells us that rainfall has nothing to do with behaviour, and Jesus agreed: he said that God sends rain (and drought) equally on the just and unjust (Matthew 5:45).

However, the first Christians were taught that even when things go wrong, God is with us and can turn it to good: "in all things God works for the good of those who love him" (Romans 8:28). That is, God can bring some good out of whatever happens – even out of the bad things. Some older Bibles unfortunately mask this message by translating, "God works all things for good…" which could be interpreted as, "God makes sure that only good things happen…" This interpretation is quickly proved wrong by real life – except, perhaps, for those who are very rich, very healthy and very "lucky"!

Why do bad things happen to good people? Is everyone, including Christians, subject to "bad luck" (i.e. random disasters)? The Bible doesn't ultimately answer this, but we do learn that God is with us in all things. Paul pointed out that we live in a fallen world marred by sin, which is groaning in pain until Jesus comes, so we shouldn't be surprised that things go wrong (Romans 8:19–25). God can gloriously bring good out of evil, but that doesn't mean he wanted the evil thing to occur.

Ever since Adam introduced disobedience and other evils, our lives have been different to what God intended. He wanted us to live for ever, in Eden, and so we can't ever complain that "God wanted this bad thing to happen to me." However, despite our disobedience, the world isn't out of God's control. He can always help us through a bad time and he can turn each bad experience into a growth point and a blessing. God is still in charge because even though the world is fallen, he is still able to achieve his will by bringing good out of evil. The cross is the ultimate example of this – the ultimate evil being turned by God into the ultimate good.

The cross was not a matter of chance. God decided to rescue a planetful of people and he did so. Whether chance or human freedom exist or not, God will do what he wishes to do. So perhaps wishing someone "Good luck" *is* scandalously pagan, because this blessing is addressed to Lady Luck, not to God!

God-sent Disasters

When Benjamin Franklin invented the lightning rod in 1752, the Pope recommended it, but many churches refused to fit one. They believed that it interfered with God's sovereign right to strike down sinners. Instead, they continued with the practice of ringing the church bells during lightning storms to call people to pray and to ward off the lightning. Unfortunately this resulted in many bell-ringers being killed by lightning – an average of three a year in Germany (where, for some reason, they kept a count). However, in 1769 the church of Saint Nazaire in Brescia, Italy, was struck by lightning which ignited the gunpowder stored in its large dry underground vaults – about 100 tons! The explosion killed 3,000 people and destroyed a sixth of the town. After this, most churches quickly fitted lighting rods to their spires.

The concept of an "act of God" started with the Laws of Hammurabi, a Babylonian law code of about 4,000 years ago. Law 249 stated that if a man hired an ox and a god struck it with lightning, he did not have to pay compensation. Today, only insurance brokers refer to lightning as an "act of God", although when lightning caused a serious fire at York Minster in 1984, many people related it to the installation of the controversial new Bishop of Durham held there three days earlier. Some newspapers had reported that the Bishop didn't believe in the resurrection. Was God agreeing with them and making his feelings known in this way?

In the meantime, the Haitian earthquake of 2010 left 316,000 people dead and 1.6 million homeless, and the Indian

Ocean tsunami of 2004 resulted in 230,000 deaths and 1.7 million homeless. Every year brings more disasters to our TV screens and, as we watch the suffering of so many, the question stays the same: "Why?"

Today, as in New Testament times, the scandal is that God gets blamed for killing apparently innocent people using natural disasters. Jesus was asked about the collapse of a tower in Siloam – a recent disaster that had killed eighteen people. And, although not a "natural" disaster, the killing of innocent bystanders by Roman soldiers in the Temple (Luke 13:1) was another event that prompted many questions as to why. The victims of both incidents didn't appear to have done anything wrong, so why did God kill them? Does God use such disasters to punish those who have secret sins?

Old Testament stories such as the destruction of Sodom or the earthquake in King Uzziah's day suggest that God does use earthy disasters as punishment. But were these disasters initiated by God in order to do his will or were they going to happen anyway and God *used* them to carry out his will? The Bible accounts suggest the second option: God makes use of natural disasters which would happen anyway; he doesn't initiate them in order to punish us.

Sodom's destruction is portrayed in the Bible as a natural disaster which God "used" as a punishment. When God spoke to Abraham about what was to happen, he said to Abraham that he would rescue everyone in the city if enough of them were righteous. Although we're not told how they would be rescued, presumably it would be the same way as Lot – by evacuation. God isn't pictured as having his hand on the plunger, just waiting until Lot is safe before he depresses it. The urgency of the angels who dragged Lot's family out of the city suggests that they had no control over the timing of the disaster (Genesis 19:15–17). It was a natural event that was going to happen whether the angels were ready or not. It was already on its way, and the angels knew it couldn't be delayed.

When an earthquake shook the kingdoms of Israel and Judah in about 760 BC, the fact that Amos had prophesied about God's judgment just two years previously made people assume that God deliberately chose to send it. But there are good reasons to doubt this. Judah's king, Uzziah (a.k.a. Azariah), was generally good (though he did bad things later, after the quake) and his people were no worse than previous generations (2 Kings 15:3–4). And although Israel's king, Jeroboam, was labelled as "bad", in fact all Israel's kings were given that title (unlike Judah, which had some "good" kings) and Jeroboam was actually better than most because God used him to rescue the people (2 Kings 14:26–27). What was new during their reigns was wealth. The wise foreign policy of both kings made a lot of people rich (see 2 Chronicles 26:8–10; 2 Kings 14:25) and Amos complained that they didn't care about those who remained poor (Amos 2:6–8). Perhaps that's why Amos specified that the "palaces" would be destroyed – though by fire and enemies, not by an earthquake (2:5; 3:11, 15).

Amos concluded: "When disaster comes to a city, has not the Lord sent it?" (Amos 3:6). He was saying that all things, good and bad, come from God, and we should listen to what God says. Of course, God wants all generations to listen to him, but this particular generation had a special chance to hear him. By giving Amos this prophecy shortly before a natural disaster occurred, God got their complete attention. He used this event to present his timeless message in a way that would be remembered and acted on. Amos' generation wasn't worse than others, but they heard a warning which we should all heed.

When Jesus was asked about the disasters in his day, his

conclusion was similar: those who suffered weren't worse sinners than anyone else and, unless you repent, you too will all perish (Luke 13:2–3). Whoa! Not exactly a comforting message to hear! And what about the innocent who suffer? Jesus said that, in effect, there aren't any innocent people because we are all sinners. These little disasters will be nothing compared to the judgment that will come to everyone. He didn't acknowledge any surprise that people were killed in these disasters – in a wicked and fallen world we should expect this kind of thing to happen. He implied that the surprising – and amazing – thing is that we sinners should experience any *good* in this world.

Jesus taught that we are all evil, but despite this the love for us in his voice is unmistakable. He said: "You don't give a stone to your children when they ask for bread, even though you are evil" (Matthew 7:9–11). Another time, when someone politely called him "good rabbi", he pointed out that only God can really be called "good". He didn't want anyone to forget that compared to God, we are all fundamentally evil. We all need God's forgiveness, even if we do good things most of the time.

Jesus shocks us by calling us evil – all of us. But why should we be shocked? We may do good things, but that doesn't mean we don't do bad things as well. Criminals in prison may well have done good things in their lives, but that doesn't stop them being punished for their crimes. Jesus merely reminds us what we're really like. The real shock is that despite this, he offers us God's forgiveness (Mark 2:5–11) and tells us that God's longing to do good for us is much more than our longing to do good for our own children (Matthew 7:9–11).

The mystery of natural disasters is not that God allows evil to happen to good people. Jesus said that the real mystery of suffering is that there is so little of it. We experience so much undeserved good that we complain when things go wrong. In our fallen world there will always be disasters and relatively good people will suffer alongside relatively bad people. But those who listen to Jesus will find a salutary reminder in those disasters. It is a reminder that a real judgment is coming which will be totally just and that God offers an eternity without evil for those who turn to him in repentance.

Unforgivable Blasphemy

Europeans have almost forgotten what blasphemy means. No one, for instance, predicted the offence and riots that were caused by cartoons featuring the prophet Mohammed in a Danish newspaper in 2005. Muslims are zealously concerned with God's honour; they would never place a Quran or a Bible on the floor, let alone use God's name inappropriately. And yet most non-Muslims rarely get through one conversation without misusing a sacred name. The UK laws against blasphemy were repealed as recently as 2008, by which time they already appeared hopelessly archaic. It seems amazing that as recently as 1977, the publisher of *Gay News* was imprisoned for describing Jesus as "well hung". The fact that I can quote these same words shows how much society has changed.

In Jesus' day, blasphemy was perhaps the most scandalous offence anyone could be accused of. Even Romans regarded impiety against the gods as an offence against the whole of society. The ancient unwritten "common law" of Rome (the *mos maiorum*) established the honour of the gods at the heart of Roman law.

Jews were so horrified by this offence that Paul and his fellow Jews were able to provoke a crowd into stoning Stephen for it. They were merely angry when Stephen accused all Jews of disobeying the law of Moses, but when he claimed that he could see "the Son of Man standing at the right hand of God", they boiled over into murderous rage (Acts 7:53–58). Many in that crowd must have remembered that Jesus had regularly referred to himself as the "Son of Man" and so the blasphemy was clear.

Jesus himself was almost stoned on a couple of occasions when he claimed that "My father and I are one" and when he said, "Before Abraham was born, I am!" (John 10:30–39; 8:58–59). The rather stilted phrase "I am" was a deliberate reference to God's interpretation of his own name, Yahweh or Jehovah – no one knows how it was really pronounced (Exodus 3:14). John's Gospel mentioned many occasions when Jesus provocatively used the phrase "I am".

John isn't alone in recording Jesus' scandalous claim to godhead because Jesus accepts similar charges of blasphemy elsewhere (Mark 2:7; 14:62–64). His most audacious claim to divinity goes almost unnoticed by modern readers, when he said: "Where two or three are gathered in my name, I am in their midst" (Matthew 18:20). Any first-century Jew would immediately recognize that Jesus was referring to a famous rabbinic saying: "When two or three sit to study Scripture, the Shekhinah is in their midst".[1] When he quotes this saying, Jesus replaced the words "the Shekhinah" (i.e. "the glory of God's presence") with "I" – something that would have been regarded as blasphemous by any Jew.

The Monty Python film *Life of Brian* is, surprisingly, one of the most accurate portrayals of life in Jesus' day (as well as one of the most amusing), but it is wrong in one respect at least: no one would get stoned simply for saying "Jehovah". In fact, in Jesus' day, people still greeted each other with "Jehovah bless you".[2] However, soon after Jesus' day, Jews did stop speaking God's actual name and replaced it with *Adonai* ("Lord") or *ha shem* ("the Name"). Modern Jewish software often says: "Please treat this printout with respect because it may contain the name of G*d."

The prohibition of blasphemy was the most serious of the Ten Commandments because it is the only one that is followed by: "The Lord will not leave this unpunished" (Exodus 20:7). The Jews concluded from this that blasphemy must be unforgivable because if God said that it would not go unpunished it meant that no amount of repentance would enable people to escape punishment by obtaining forgiveness.

Jesus didn't repeal this law – he actually extended it in a surprising way. When some Pharisees accused him of casting out demons by Satan's power, he replied by accusing them of blasphemy: "whoever blasphemes the Holy Spirit never has forgiveness" (Matthew 12:26–32). Jesus had already pointed out the obvious: Satan's demons weren't being cast out by Satan's power, so this must have been the work of the Holy Spirit. He therefore accused the Pharisees of equating the Holy Spirit with Satan and said this was unforgivable blasphemy.

The Jews weren't surprised to hear that blasphemy was unforgivable – they already knew this from the Ten Commandments. The shock was that Jesus said blasphemy against the *Holy Spirit* was unforgivable. Since the law said only that blasphemy against God was unforgivable, it meant that Jesus was putting the Holy Spirit on a par with God!

Jesus reinforced this conclusion by reminding them that "blasphemy" is forgivable when it is directed at anyone except God. At this point our English language gets in the way of understanding what Jesus means because in English we "insult" people and "blaspheme" God, whereas Greek uses the same word for "insults" directed at both people and God. For example, when Jews "insulted" Paul, the Greek verb used is *blasphémeo* (Acts 13:45; 18.6). Jesus' saying becomes clearer if we translate it as: "all insults will be forgiven but insults against the Holy Spirit will never be forgiven" (Mark 3:28–29). By pointing out that this insult is unforgivable, Jesus defined it as an insult against God – that is, he was implying that the Holy Spirit *is* God.

Jesus added that "speaking against the Son of Man is forgivable" (Matthew 12:32). This is surprising because, as we have seen, the Gospels weren't shy to proclaim Jesus' divinity. We must therefore assume that he did not class this as the ultimate sin because his divinity was not yet obvious; however, after the resurrection, such doubt was no longer an excuse. The letter to the Hebrews points out the seriousness of reviling Jesus and says: "there no longer remains a sacrifice for sins" after such rejection (Hebrews 6:4–6; 10:26–29). The reason why their sin cannot be forgiven is because they know who Jesus is yet still choose not to turn to him in repentance. The only unforgivable sin is that which is unrepented before Jesus – because he is the only source of forgiveness.

The Jews believed that God forgave minor sins immediately after repentance, but major sins remained unforgiven until the sacrifice given on the next Day of Atonement. But what about blasphemy? How could that be forgiven when God had said it would not go unpunished? In the early second century Rabbi Ishmael ben Elisha "solved" that problem by saying that death was sufficient punishment – that is, if you repented, God would forgive your blasphemy at your death. Forgiveness wasn't so complicated for Christians, because Jesus' sacrifice covers all punishments and enables him to offer immediate forgiveness for any repented sin – even the sin of blasphemy.

The real tragedy of the "unforgivable sin" is that many people who suffer from psychological feelings of guilt assume that they must have committed a sin which can't be forgiven. Their conviction of guilt is so overwhelming that they *feel* unforgivable. This is compounded when they read in Hebrews that forgiveness is impossible for those who deliberately choose to reject God.

However, the very fact that someone wants to repent and be reconciled with God is proof that they have not irrevocably decided to reject him. God is always ready to receive a sinner, and Jesus died for every sin. The letter to the Hebrews is very clear: for those who reject Jesus' sacrifice, there is no other source of forgiveness. This doesn't mean that the rejection itself is an unforgivable sin, but it emphasizes that Jesus is the *only* source of forgiveness. If you reject Jesus' sacrifice, there is nothing left. But if you have the longing to repent, this demonstrates that you have not ultimately decided to reject Jesus – and God's arms, like the arms of the Prodigal's father, always remain open to welcome you.

Notes

1. Mishnah Avot 3.6 – "two or three" comes from the discussion immediately following this saying. Both sayings are clearly related to each other, and the original version must have been the Jewish one, because Jews wouldn't have adapted a saying by Jesus.
2. Mishnah Berakhot 9.5.

Eternal Torment

"It's not fair" is an all-too-familiar little phrase that children use before they learn that life simply *isn't* fair. What begins as a cry for justice turns into a resigned silence – or sometimes even a quest for personal revenge. Of course, we try to explain to them that God will bring real justice… but then they learn the church's teaching on hell and discover that all sin results in the same punishment. A shoplifter who doesn't repent will be punished in exactly the same way as a multiple rapist or murderer who doesn't repent. Like Abraham, we'd love to say to God: "Far be this from you! Surely the Judge of all the earth will act justly?" (Genesis 18:25). We want to shout out to him: "It's not fair!"

Common Jewish teaching about hell in the time of Jesus is illustrated in a parable told by a rabbi called Johanan ben Zakkai. He is significant because his forty-year ministry in Galilee overlapped with the time when Jesus was preaching and teaching, and Jesus is likely to have heard Johanan himself tell the parable. Johanan was probably passing on a familiar story, one that Jesus' listeners would all know:

> A king invited all his people to a banquet but did not say when it would start. The wise people put on their fine clothes and waited at the door of the palace saying, "Surely a royal palace already has everything ready." The foolish people carried on with their work saying, "Surely a banquet takes time to prepare." Suddenly the king called in the people; the wise entered in fine clothes but the foolish entered in dirty

clothes. The king rejoiced at the wise but was angry with the fools. He ordered: "Let those who dressed for the banquet sit and feast, but those who did not dress for the banquet will stand and watch them."[1]

This parable reflected the common Jewish theology that all Jews would go to heaven, but they would not all receive equal honour – the fools didn't share the honour (i.e. the food) that the wise enjoyed.

Hell was an important part of Jesus' teaching. In fact, he taught more about it than any other Jew of his time – the Gospels record forty-five verses on hell, which is a large number when compared with the sixty-five verses on love. Jesus replied to Johanan's teaching by telling similar parables of his own – people being invited to a king's banquet, the wise and foolish girls waiting to join a wedding party, and the man thrown out of a banquet for not being dressed properly (Matthew 22:2–14; 25:1–13 and parallels in the other Gospels). In each of these, he contradicted Johanan's well-known parable in one important way: many people are *excluded* from the banquet – they aren't ready and arrive too late, after the doors are closed; they decide themselves not to go; or they are thrown out.

Jesus had to speak about hell so much because he disagreed fundamentally about it with almost all other Jews. Jesus told them that unless they personally repented, they were all going to hell (Luke 13:28). This was utterly scandalous to most Jews.

Many people today are equally scandalized by Jesus' teaching but for a different reason: the eternal punishment of hell seems disproportionate for all but a few utterly evil people. It is a subject that we do not often hear preached on today – perhaps because it is so offensive to most people.

Jesus was very clear about the fate of those left "outside"

the banquet. He said there would be "weeping and gnashing of teeth" – that is, the suffering of hell (Matthew 22:13; compare with Matthew 13:42, 50). He described hell in exactly the same way as other Jews by likening it to a place called Gehenna where there was everlasting fire and worms. No one thought that this was a literal description of hell because they knew it couldn't be – they had all been to the actual place: Gehenna was the name of a local garbage dump in a valley south of Jerusalem. Later rabbis said that rubbish was burned there continuously, though the thing it was most remembered for was that it was the place where babies were once burned to death as sacrifices on the altars of Molech (2 Kings 23:10). The worms (i.e. maggots) were just as literal – they were everywhere among the rotting garbage. Everyone referred to hell as "Gehenna", because Gehenna was such a ghastly place.

Is the real hell like that – with fire and maggots? If it is, then presumably heaven consists of millions of "mansions" filled with the sound of "harpers harping with their harps" (in the wonderful language of the King James version at John 14:2 and Revelation 14:2). Thankfully these are only pictures or metaphors of something we can't describe – harp music for eternity sounds hellish to me! The "fire and maggots" terminology was not specially chosen by Jesus – everyone described hell like that. He used the same imagery because he agreed with the ideas it expressed – that hell was an appalling place.

Is the punishment of hell eternal? Some Jews in Jesus' day thought that most people would spend only a short time in hell. They believed there were three groups of people: the righteous, the evil, and the in-betweens (i.e. the majority). The righteous would go straight to heaven and the evil to hell, but the in-betweens would drop to hell, squeal in the fire, and jump up to heaven.[2] This idea didn't catch on, but it resulted in making other Jews define more precisely what eternal punishment meant. Here's a very clear description from one of the Dead Sea Scrolls:

> The judgment of all who walk in such ways will be multiple afflictions at the hand of all the angels of perdition, everlasting damnation in the wrath of God's furious vengeance, never-ending terror and reproach for all eternity, with a shameful extinction in the fire of Hell's outer darkness. For all their eras, generation by generation, they will know doleful sorrow, bitter evil and dark happenstance, until their utter destruction with neither remnant nor rescue.[3]

We can see that they definitely believed that the punishment of hell was eternal and Jesus agreed with this. Even though there is only one verse in the Gospels where he clearly said that punishment is eternal (Matthew 25:46), it doesn't mean that he didn't teach it – he just didn't need to emphasize this aspect because most Jews already believed it. Jesus also alluded to eternal punishment by frequently using the terminology in which this teaching was normally expressed (see, for example, the language in the above quote from Qumran). Throughout all strands of the Gospels he spoke about "fire" which he described as "eternal", and he constantly referred to "weeping and teeth-clenching pain" (Matthew 5:22; 7:19; 8:12, 41, 50; 13:40; 18:8; 22:13; 24:51; 25:30, 41; Mark 9:43, 48; Luke 13:28; John 15:6). By using the familiar terminology that his listeners associated with descriptions of eternal punishment, Jesus showed that he affirmed this teaching.

What kind of punishment happens in hell? Is it eternal torment or eternal destruction? In other words, is hell like a sentence of permanent imprisonment or is it like a sentence of execution (which is equally permanent)? The word "punishment" (*kolasis*) in Matthew 25:46 can refer to "torment" or "destruction" or both,[4] so it isn't obvious how to translate exactly what Jesus meant here. You could argue that "fire" has the function of destroying trash, so that hell must be a place where evil is destroyed. But you could also argue that the flames are special ones that inflict pain without destroying, so that hell must be a place of eternal torment. These arguments merely demonstrate how careful we have to be when basing conclusions on metaphors.

Some theologians say that Jesus meant "eternal torment" and others say he meant "destruction" (i.e. annihilation). Both groups are right. The Gospels often refer to the terrible torment of hell (Matthew 8:12; 13:42, 50; 22:13; 24:51; 25:30; Luke 13:28), but they *also* refer to "destruction" (*apollumi*), which is also translated "perishing" – for example, "whoever believes in him shall not perish but have eternal life" (John 3:16; see also Matthew 10:28; 18:14). The concept of "destruction" in hell is also found in the rest of the New Testament – for example, "they will be punished with everlasting destruction" (2 Thessalonians 1:9; see also Romans 9:22; James 4:12). Both interpretations of "eternal punishment" can be true if the punishment of hell involves torment followed by destruction (though it means that the torment suffered must be for a limited time). Jesus' listeners wouldn't have been surprised by this dual aspect of punishment, because the Jewish passage quoted above similarly spoke of "terror" followed by "extinction" and "doleful sorrow" followed by "utter destruction".

How long are people tormented in hell? Unlike the gruesome imagery of some rabbis and preachers, Jesus didn't speak about those in hell spending millennia being prodded by toasting forks in boiling faeces. Instead he told a parable which implies that suffering will be proportional to guilt. He said: a master returned unexpectedly and when he found his chief servant drunk and other servants misbehaving, the master punished them. Different servants received different amounts of punishment: "The servant who knows the master's will and does not get ready or does not do what the master wants will be beaten with many blows. But the one who does not know, and does things deserving punishment will be beaten with few blows" (Luke 12:47–48). Jesus was clearly talking about hell, because they were also "assigned a place with the unbelievers" (v. 46).

This amazing parable tells us not only that suffering in hell will be proportional to the amount of evil committed, but also that it will be proportional to how much the person understood about right and wrong. If they definitely knew their actions were wrong, they will suffer more than if they merely acted thoughtlessly and without deliberation. For the Jews this kind of teaching was utterly scandalous because it suggested that Jews (who knew the most about what God wanted) would be punished more severely than the Gentiles! But Jesus was absolutely clear: the Jews would not go to heaven simply by being born Jews.

Jesus' teaching about hell was both frightening and fair. Punishment in hell is eternal – there is no release after a period of torment because it also involves eternal destruction. However, the amount of torment is proportional to the amount of sin and guilt, because the person who did what they knew God had forbidden was considered more guilty. The devil and his angels, who know exactly what they are doing, will be tormented for eternity (Revelation 20:10), but most humans are much less evil.

God is infinitely less simplistic in his judgment than some theologians are. He takes account of how much evil we commit and how much we know about it – ignorance is, at least, a partial defence before God. This means that God's justice is more sophisticated and fair than any human court can be. In the end, we can agree with Abraham: "Surely the Judge of all the earth *will* act justly!"

Notes

1. Babylonian Talmud 153a.
2. Tosepheta Sanhedrin 13.3.
3. *Rule of the Community* 4.12–14.
4. For example in 4 Maccabees 8:9 it means "torment" but in 2 Maccabees 4:38 it means "destruction". In Wisdom 19.4 it means both, because it describes the dual "punishment" of the Egyptian army by the torments of the plagues and destruction at the Red Sea.

Further Reading

On the cultural background of the New Testament:

Mark Harding, ed., *Early Christian Life and Thought in Social Context: A Reader*, New York: T&T Clark, 2003.
– a useful collection of the important sources with some brief explanations.

David Instone-Brewer, *Traditions of the Rabbis from the Era of the New Testament* (Grand Rapids, Mich: William B. Eerdmans, 2004).
– an in-depth exploration of the rabbinic sources from the times of the Gospels.

James F. Jeffers, *The Greco-Roman World of the New Testament Era: Exploring the Background of Early Christianity* (Downers Grove, Illinois: InterVarsity Press, 1999).
– clear summaries of what we know about Roman society in Jesus' day.

On New Testament ethics in the context of the times:

Richard B. Hays, *The Moral Vision of the New Testament: Community, Cross, New Creation. A Contemporary Introduction to New Testament Ethics* (Edinburgh: T & T Clark, 1997)
– both the theory and practical examples of how to extract ethics from and ancient text.

David Instone-Brewer, *Divorce and Remarriage in the Bible: The*

Social and Literary Context (Grand Rapids, Mich: William B. Eerdmans, 2002).

– how to apply cultural context in order to understand Bible ethics for today.

On the historicity of the Gospels:

Richard Bauckham, *Jesus and the Eyewitnesses: The Gospels as Eyewitness Testimony* (Grand Rapids, Mich: William B. Eerdmans, 2006).

– solid scholarship which argues that the Gospels were based on eyewitness reports.

Craig S. Keener, *The Historical Jesus of the Gospels* (Grand Rapids, Mich: Eerdmans, 2009).

– pulls together a multitude of studies in support of historical facts behind the Gospels.

Craig A. Evans. *Fabricating Jesus: How Modern Scholars Distort the Gospels* (Nottingham: Inter-Varsity Press, 2007).

– how historians subject the Gospels to much more scrutiny than other ancient texts.

Index